THE POLITICAL ECONOMY OF DIET, HEALTH AND FOOD POLICY

Governments and individuals are becoming increasingly aware of the physical and political implications of what we eat. *The Political Economy of Diet, Health and Food Policy* discusses food in relation to public health policy. Continuing the exploration of food systems undertaken in the highly acclaimed *Consumption in the Age of Affluence: The World of Food*, this volume offers a provocative critique of traditional food systems theory and existing approaches to food consumption.

Deploying an interdisciplinary approach rooted in political economy, the author develops a unique perspective on diet, health and policy issues. It is argued that patterns of food consumption and choice can only be understood in relation to specific foods and the chains of activities and processes that surround them. These principles inform the incisive discussion of a number of food problems, including eating disorders and diseases of affluence, the contradictions of the food information system and the relationship between European Union agricultural policy and food policy.

The author concludes with a critical assessment of the UK government's newly published proposals to set up an independent food standards agency. Unique in offering a coherent picture of what we eat and why, and how food policy is responding to this, this volume will be a valuable contribution to the new and vital discipline of food studies. It will be of interest to students of political economy, food studies and the social sciences.

Ben Fine is Professor of Economics and Director of the Centre for Economic Policy for South Africa at the School of Oriental and African Studies, University of London. Recent books include *The World of Consumption* (Routledge, 1993) and *Consumption in the Age of Affluence: The World of Food* (Routledge, 1996).

ROUTLEDGE FRONTIERS OF POLITICAL ECONOMY

1 EQUILIBRIUM VERSUS UNDERSTANDING
Towards the rehumanization of economics within social theory
Mark Addleson

2 EVOLUTION, ORDER AND COMPLEXITY
Edited by Elias L. Khalil and Kenneth E. Boulding

3 INTERACTIONS IN POLITICAL ECONOMY
Malvern after ten years
Edited by Steven Pressman

4 THE END OF ECONOMICS
Michael Perelman

5 PROBABILITY IN ECONOMICS
Omar F. Hamouda and Robin Rowley

6 CAPITAL CONTROVERSY, POST KEYNESIAN
ECONOMICS AND THE HISTORY OF ECONOMICS
Essays in honour of Geoff Harcourt, Volume One
Edited by Philip Arestis, Gabriel Palma and Malcolm Sawyer

7 MARKETS, UNEMPLOYMENT AND ECONOMIC POLICY
Essays in honour of Geoff Harcourt, Volume Two
Edited by Philip Arestis, Gabriel Palma and Malcolm Sawyer

8 SOCIAL ECONOMY
The logic of capitalist development
Clark Everling

9 NEW KEYNESIAN ECONOMICS/POST-KEYNESIAN
ALTERNATIVES
Edited by Roy J. Rotheim

10 THE REPRESENTATIVE AGENT IN MACROECONOMICS
James E. Hartley

11 BORDERLANDS OF ECONOMICS
Essays in honour of Daniel R. Fusfeld
Edited by Nahid Aslanbeigui and Young Back Choi

12 VALUE DISTRIBUTION AND CAPITAL
Edited by Gary Mongiovi and Fabio Petri

13 THE ECONOMICS OF SCIENCE
Methodology and epistemology as if economics really mattered
James R. Wible

14 COMPETITIVENESS, LOCALIZED LEARNING AND
REGIONAL DEVELOPMENT
Specialization and prosperity in small open economies
*Peter Maskell, Heikki Eskelinen, Ingjaldur Hannibalsson, Anders Malmberg and
Eirik Vatne*

15 LABOUR MARKET THEORY
A constructive reassessment
Ben Fine

16 WOMEN AND EUROPEAN EMPLOYMENT
Jill Rubery, Mark Smith, Colette Fagan and Damian Grimshaw

17 EXPLORATIONS IN ECONOMIC METHODOLOGY
From Lakatos to empirical philosophy of science
Roger Backhouse

18 SUBJECTIVITY IN POLITICAL ECONOMY
Essays on wanting and choosing
David P. Levine

19 THE POLITICAL ECONOMY OF MIDDLE EAST PEACE
The impact of competing Arab and Israeli trade
Edited by J. W. Wright, Jnr

20 THE ACTIVE CONSUMER
Novelty and surprise in consumer choice
Edited by Marina Bianchi

21 SUBJECTIVISM AND ECONOMIC ANALYSIS
Essays in memory of Ludwig Lachmann
Edited by Roger Koppl and Gary Mongiovi

22 THEMES IN POST-KEYNESIAN ECONOMICS
Essays in honour of Geoff Harcourt, Volume Three
Edited by Peter Kriesler and Claudio Sardoni

23 THE DYNAMICS OF TECHNOLOGICAL KNOWLEDGE
Cristiano Antonelli

24 THE POLITICAL ECONOMY OF DIET, HEALTH AND
FOOD POLICY
Ben Fine

THE POLITICAL ECONOMY OF DIET, HEALTH AND FOOD POLICY

Ben Fine

London and New York

First published 1998
by Routledge
11 New Fetter Lane, London EC4P 4EE

Simultaneously published in the USA and Canada
by Routledge
29 West 35th Street, New York, NY 10001

© 1998 Ben Fine

Typeset in Garamond by Routledge
Printed and bound in Great Britain by Clays Ltd, St Ives plc

British Library Cataloguing in Publication Data
A catalogue record for this book is available from the British Library

Library of Congress Cataloguing in Publication Data
A catalogue record for this book has been requested

ISBN 0–415–16366–8

CONTENTS

1 **Introduction and overview**   1
   Introduction   1
   Overview   9

2 **Resolving the diet paradox**   13
   Introduction   13
   The organic content of food   18
   Does Engel's Law really apply to food?   24
   Concluding remarks   27

3 **The political economy of eating disorders**   28
   Introduction   28
   Why political economy?   31
   What are eating disorders?   35
   From sociocultural to socioeconomic approaches   43
   Why food?   48
   Why thinness? Contradictions in the political economy
     of body image   53
   Concluding observations   57

4 **Digesting the food and information systems**   58
   Introduction   58
   The food information system and trickle-down of knowledge   62
   What role is to be played by nutritional education?   68
   The good, the bad, the commercial and the non-commercial   76
   Collaboration between nutritionists and commerce?   79
   The unfolding of healthy eating   82

CONTENTS

Towards an alternative   88
Concluding remarks   92

5 **Agricultural support and diet**   96
   Introduction   96
   CAP and the nation's diet   97
   *Lessons from the Norwegian experience: the exception
       that proves the rule*   108

6 **Whither food policy?**   116

   Notes   121
   References   138
   Index   161

1

INTRODUCTION AND OVERVIEW

Introduction

The world of food looks very different today than it did at the beginning of the century, let alone at the beginning of the millennium. Perhaps, however, the appropriate comparison is with the concerns of the nineteenth century, when, inspired by the dire predictions of Malthusianism, even the prospects of what is now the developed world seemed to be doomed to an inadequate supply of food to feed the mounting population. Whilst it remains true that a substantial minority of the world's population is inadequately fed, agricultural productivity has outstripped population growth. There is enough food to feed the world.

In this light, there has been a corresponding shift in what is perceived to be the food problem. As a starting point, it is worth observing that, from a historical perspective, the food problem looks very different whether looking forward or backwards. Looking forward from the past tends to dictate a focus upon growing supply – how to feed the growing needs of a growing population – including the provision of a sufficient surplus both to source the raw materials of industrialisation and to nourish the standard of living of the non-farming workforce. Looking back, at least from a UK or western perspective, it is no longer a problem of insufficient food or the inadequacy of supply. This does remain a problem for large numbers in the third world. But, even there, as recent debates about famine have indicated, there is more to food than supply, with the need to pay attention to access or entitlement to food irrespective of absolute levels of supply.[1] Starvation exists alongside plenty, most strikingly, for example, in the greater grain consumption by cattle than humans in order to meet the diets of western affluence.[2]

1

One unsurprising consequence of the conquest of food shortage is that attention should shift away from the *dual* historical focus upon the *supply* of a *staple* food to, at the other extreme, a contemporary concern with consumer *demand* across a *variety* of foods. This change in emphasis towards food choice raises questions that need to be answered even in the historically forward-looking perspective. For there have always been a variety of foods produced and consumed, both within and across countries and over time. It is necessary to investigate why staples should have become so, or customary, and not simply to presume that this can be taken as given for reasons of tradition, climate or whatever. It is a matter of what foods as well as of how much and how they are distributed and used. The study of food in the past, or in the context of malnutrition in the present, must not be confined to questions of supply.

Such a perspective is uncontroversial in moving from the past to the present for affluent societies. It is not so much a question of shifting attention from supply to demand or choice as to how to do it. The volume to which this is a sequel, Fine *et al.* (1996), attempted to provide an answer to this question.[3] It is worth giving a brief account of the origins of that study in order to clarify the basis for this book. Five years or so ago, a research team of Michael Heasman, Judith Wright and myself began a project under the ESRC's Nation's Diet Programme. To oversimplify and verge on parody, the programme had been initiated in order to understand food choice in the UK diet and how it might be improved in view of the diseases of affluence – too much food of the wrong type, leading to unnecessary illness and premature death. As nutritional advice had apparently failed to convince the general public to eat more healthily, social scientists were to be supported in their endeavour to explain, and possibly advise on how to change, the nation's diet.

Our own study within this programme of research had three components.[4] First, it involved an empirical investigation of shifting food 'norms' for a selection of foods, especially those for which there had been changes in consumption. The data used drew upon the National Food Survey (NFS) from between 1975 and 1990. The NFS is an annual survey of 7,000 or so households, reporting on food purchases as well as a variety of socioeconomic characteristics. The data were used to calculate food norms, by which we meant systematic patterns of consumption across households, taking into account the variation in socioeconomic variables such as household composition, age of family members, income level, class, and so on.

The calculation of food norms allowed some of the proximate correlates of food choices to be identified. But how are these to be explained? The second component of our research involved moving away from the consumer and choice in order to examine food systems as a whole, by which is meant the chain of activity from farm to mouth. What is a food system, how does it function, what makes it change, and so on? Third, the attempt was then made to bring the other two components together and explain the patterns of proximate food choice by reference to the systems of food provision.

Rather than repeat the analytical findings that continue to inform this volume, what follows is a drastic and selective summary of the results, supplemented by some reference to the literature that has appeared since the first volume. As a first proposition, it is essential to examine food provision within the analytical framework provided by a theory of food systems. The latter includes an understanding of the socioeconomic structures by which processes are undertaken from agriculture through to consumption, thereby including the roles played by landed property, technology, industry, distribution, wholesaling and retailing, as well as the material culture surrounding consumption such as the creation of meanings and activities around food.

To some extent, such a conclusion is uncontroversial and even taken unthinkingly for granted, especially now that there are concerns about the environmental and ethical implications of modern agriculture, over-use of chemicals and bio-technology respectively, and the health and safety content of modern food supply. To know what we eat and with what effects, we cannot rest upon a study of food choice unconnected with how food is provided. For example, Tansey and Worsley (1995) have provided a justifiably welcome account of 'the food system', aptly subtitled *A Guide*. Their approach, as does any based upon the notion of a food system, has the considerable strength of incorporating the potential to address any factor along the food chain that is of importance in cause or effect even if it is not immediately apparent in the products taken down from the supermarket shelf or spooned from the table.

By the same token, the descriptive scope of a food system approach can render it unrooted analytically. How do we identify what belongs to a food system and what does not? How and why does a food system change? Our second proposition addresses such conundrums directly. It argues that there are a variety of food systems which are quite distinct from one another, whether from one country to another, from one product or group of products to another within the same country, or over time. For example, for the UK, our research identified distinct and distinctive dairy systems, meat systems (but not separate systems for poultry, beef and pork at the moment) and sugar systems (itself separate from the 'artificial' sweetener system). Analytically and empirically, it is essential to examine how such systems have been created or structured and how they have developed by being restructured, reproduced and/or transformed.

For the moment, it suffices to suggest that there are distinct food systems whose scope and content is filled out historically. Proceeding with some hesitation, an analogy might be helpful. What do we mean by a nation? It has various components, of which one is territorial integrity. Starting with the notion of a system of nation-states, it is possible to argue that how these are formed, and with what content, is a historical process. Similarly, the food system is itself made up of a number of constituent food systems, each with its own scope and content.

Consider, for example, Wells' (1996) study of the strawberry system,[5] although her concern is with working conditions and workers' organisation and protest rather than food choice. In order to address these issues, she concludes more generally: 'The commodities, technologies, production processes, and input and product markets of particular industries shape the interests, opportunities, and capacities of social classes' (p. 282). She continues: 'The present study and others attest that the progress of industrialisation and globalisation in agriculture is highly uneven, and that the structures of agricultural commodity systems remain remarkably heterogeneous' (p. 308). Thus, they should be analysed as such. A similar conclusion is implicit in the study of sugar by Bonnano *et al.* (1995) in the context of the relative power of a transnational corporation, Ferruzzi, and the nation-state, and in the comparative study of the Australian and US dairy systems provided by Pritchard (1996). For Strak and Morgan (eds) (1995), an overview of the UK food and drink industry naturally falls into a sector-by-sector analysis of the vertically organised systems for the provision of food.

Yet it would be a mistake to suggest that the food system approach is predominant, let alone exclusive to the literature. Far more common, and continuing the fashion rapidly established in the recent popularity of food studies and of consumption more generally, many contributions have implicitly rejected the food system approach. Rather than examining the factors, 'vertically' organised in the provision of particular foods, attention has been focused upon one or, usually, more of the 'horizontal' factors common across a number of foods. This has the added convenience of allowing contributors to roam within their own academic disciplines and is especially prevalent in the analysis of food choice and meaning to consumers. For example, Caplan's (1997) study of food, health and identity points to analysis in terms of language, practices, agency, body, risk, ethnicity, class, status, gender, and so on. Beardsworth and Keil (1997) range over an even greater variety of potential explanatory factors. Warde (1997a) is more selective, choosing to focus on what he terms four antinomies of taste – novelty and tradition, health and indulgence, economy and extravagance, and care and convenience.

However, as has been recognised by others, and is implicitly acknowledged by Warde himself, this is an arbitrary privileging of some antinomies or factors as opposed to others that could be chosen. Warde's contribution is replete with other analytical scalpels, including individualisation, informalisation, communification, stylisation, cash and class, gender and time, discipline and self-surveillance, commodification, and so on. Lupton (1996), in particular, opens her book by suggesting that 'food and eating habits are banal practices of everyday life' (p. 1). She then proceeds to examine the complexity of banality. For food consumption habits, it is shown, are not to be tied simply to biological needs but serve to mark boundaries between social classes, geographic regions, nations, cultures, genders, life-festivals, seasons and times of day. Lupton is also drawn to a range of binary classifications for foods: good/bad, male/female, powerful/weak, alive/dead, healthy/unhealthy, comfort/punishment, sophisticated/gauche, sin/virtue, animal/vegetable, raw/cooked, and self/other.

It is apparent, then, as recognised by Lupton and others, that all emotions and forms of identity can be expressed through food. In this respect, it is like money or a blank analytical cheque which has the general power of purchase both for the consumer (I am what I eat) and for the social scientist (you are what my theory says you eat). Unlike money, however, food is not homogeneous;[6] it is heterogeneous and differentiated. As already suggested, in order to disentangle the unlimited web of factors that can be incorporated into food, it is essential both to differentiate between foods and to trace their provision back through their distinctive food systems.

5

This is also true of attempts to examine food at stages in the food system other than at consumption. Blaxter and Robertson (1995), for example, are concerned with the revolutions in agriculture which have paved the way for the transition from dearth to plenty. However, it is apparent that their discussion of productivity increase – in mechanisation, seed and other inputs, animals, and so on – is uneven and highly specific in impact from one food to another, both indirectly at the level of supply and indirectly elsewhere along the food chain.

Nonetheless, there is undoubtedly a lingering problem with the food systems approach adopted here, and it has been made explicit in the literature. Essentially, the problem revolves around the dual issues of what constitute the boundaries of one food system as opposed to another, and, given this, the correct notion that there are integral connections at the level of consumption between different foods (and food systems). The first issue has already been addressed here in terms of recognising that food systems themselves, both socially and historically, demarcate themselves through the reproduction or transformation of their associated socioeconomic structures. The second issue is covered in depth in Fine *et al.*, in part through debate with Glennie and Thrift over consumption more generally,[7] and in part through the specification of particular food systems attached to dairy, meat and sugar. Integration across food systems, whether at the level of consumption or not, does not undermine the notion of separate food systems. Indeed, it depends upon it for they have to be separate in order to be brought together! In any case, if two food systems are so closely integrated that they become inseparable, then they can be reinterpreted as a single food system. Whilst this stance has the whiff of tautology around it, with the capacity to accommodate any empirical outcome, it is an explicit recognition that a capitalist society is organised around commodity production and the continuing restructuring around economies of scope and scale.

Weight can be added to this debate, however, in a slightly different way in the light of Warde's (1997b) review of Fine *et al.* (1996), in which it is criticised, for example, for being unable to address the sociology of the meal and, therefore, for being of more limited general use to sociologists. This is a powerful critique of the food systems approach adopted here along the lines of food choice and consumption as integral across differentiated food systems. A meal, not least for sociologists after all, gains its substance and meaning from being more than the sum of its individual parts.

As a first response, it must be observed that an analysis based on distinct food systems does not preclude an investigation of the meal as an integral component of daily life or food studies. There can be no presumption that the meat and two veg go better together analytically because they are traditionally put together on the plate. Indeed, putting them together before they get on the plate can be one way of creating a specific food system in the form of a particular type of ready-made meal (which itself depends upon technological developments both inside and outside the home and the subversion of the meal as meat and two veg prepared by a mother and/or wife).

In short, the existence of meals as such does not in and of itself undermine a food systems approach. It is a matter of how the analysis of the meal is put together. The recognition that there is a sociology of the meal that goes beyond its separate food components does not entail an abandonment of analysis of the provision of those components. Indeed, this is imperative, otherwise causal and underlying factors in creating and defining the meanings of meals will be lost in the more or less immediate discourse of the meal itself.

Such comments are borne out by consideration of the more recent literature on the sociology of the meal. Wood (1995), for example, offers a scathing review of the 'state of the art'. He observes an unresolved tension between the macro and micro aspects – food as an expression of social constructs and daily practices of particular families, respectively. He concludes:

> It is sad, but by no means difficult, to accept that modern sociology, with its predilections for navel-contemplation and obsessions with intra-disciplinary debates, has managed largely to ignore both that phenomenon (food) and activity (eating) which are absolutely fundamental to human existence. It is tempting to observe that food is, in any case, too important a topic to be left to sociologists alone! Certainly, a multi-disciplinary approach to the topic is . . . not only desirable but largely unavoidable.
>
> (p. 125)

His own solution, however, in order to avoid analytical coarseness, is to adopt 'middle-range theory', which, in practice, is to rely upon *ad hoc* selection from grand and mundane postures.[8] How much more satisfactory to synthesise the macro and micro as well as interdisciplinary integration through analysis of the food systems that make up meals. Further, from the author who is probably most closely associated with the sociology of the meal comes the warning not to exaggerate the tradition and generality of shared family meals against the enduring claim that they are being eroded along with family values, and so on (Murcott, 1997). In short, meals are, as they have always been, as heterogeneous as the foods of which they are comprised, and a food systems approach opens that heterogeneity to investigation rather than precluding it.

So far, emphasis has been placed upon food systems and their distinctiveness. But is this all that marks food as distinctive? To return to the earlier view of the history of food as the overcoming of the scarcity of supply: does this set it apart from other items of consumption? For the history of food can be examined like any other good according to our analytical prejudices and inclinations – as, for example, shifts in supply and demand as technology and tastes change or are induced to change over time. In this context, it is worth mentioning that the food study leading to this and the earlier volume (Fine *et al.*, 1996) was preceded by a more general study of consumption (and twentieth-century 'consumer society') and the relationship between increasing female labour market participation and the purchase of labour-saving consumer durables. Analytically, the conclusion was drawn (Fine and Leopold, 1993) that consumption needs to be understood in terms of distinct systems of provision – the analytical analogue to food systems – which are integral and structurally differentiated from one another, as in housing, energy, transport or clothing systems.

As such, if there are separate food systems, this does not render them distinctive as food but only as specific items of consumption. Does anything else set food apart from other items of consumption? One answer, readily taken for granted and equally easily overlooked, is the notion that food is an irreducible necessity. But this property does not set food apart from other necessities, such as clothing and shelter. Yet it would be peculiar to view the history of clothing simply as the struggle to have enough to wear, for even cheap clothes have to be designed and made.

Closer to the mark in setting food apart from other necessities is the notion that there is something biological about food, not least in its dependence upon natural processes. Even this is not distinctive to food, for agricultural raw materials are, for example, used in a wide range of non-food production. What does set food apart, however, is the necessary presence of the 'natural' at both the beginning and the end of the food systems – both in agriculture and in palatability. Without in any way embracing any sort of naturalism

8

or biological determinism, what the previous volume termed the organic properties of food are inevitably socially defined and constructed but they are also unavoidable along the entire system of provision in a way that is not true, for example, of the chain of activities that lead to a TV set or a motor car.

In some respects, the intermediate stages between agriculture and food consumption involve the attempt to overcome or even to deploy organic properties as in preservation and standardisation of food. The third proposition, then, incorporating the other two, is that food should be studied as a number of distinct product-defined systems of provision, uniting production to consumption with a particularly important and distinctive presence of organic content. Food is grown and literally consumed.

Finally, the presentation so far has largely been analytically neutral on how food systems should be identified and examined. At one extreme, there is a longstanding descriptive tradition, with a more or less formal examination of supply and demand, possibly incorporating agriculture, technology, transport, trade, tastes, and so on. The approach adopted here is different and would emphasise:

1 vertical integration and disintegration along the food chain in the sense of the distribution and redistribution of activities and processes from farm to mouth;
2 the corresponding reproduction or transformation of structures along the food chain;
3 the importance of a full and sophisticated understanding of the role played by landed property – who gains access to the right to produce and under what conditions;
4 analytical attention to underlying tendencies, such as commodification and internationalisation, but the recognition that they co-exist with countertendencies and interact with them to give rise to complex outcomes;
5 the previous factors are crucial in identifying distinct food systems and, especially, the reasons for the role played by the state and state policy.

Overview

These propositions are developed, justified and put into practice in Fine *et al.* (1996) in providing explanation for some aspects of food choice. The current volume is much broader in scope. Chapter 2 employs the previously developed food systems theory to review some of the literature that has gathered around food studies. It is argued, in what is termed the 'diet paradox', that there is very little coherence to what is a disparate collection of contributions from a variety of disciplines, covering an even wider range of topics. There is a presumption that the study of food or diet is what unites the literature but the inevitable conclusion, for the literature taken together, is that this is merely a flag of convenience so that diet does not constitute a well-defined analytical category. Hence the paradox: diet is at least implicitly the object of study in each case but it does not exist since it is, at one and the same time, a socioeconomic category with greater analytical connections with non-food than with other food items – as in symbol, ritual, stratification, identity, and so on. The paradox is resolved, a potential place provided for food studies as a well-defined discipline, and the existing literature opened to critical assessment and incorporation, by organising it within a framework determined by two guiding questions. First, how do particular contributions shed light upon or further the study of food systems and how conscious are they of the functioning of food systems as integral unities? Second, how is the organic content of food recognised and incorporated?

Chapter 3 critically assesses the theory that has been used to examine the social and historical incidence of eating disorders. Whilst it has been recognised that anorexia, for example, derives both from the compulsion to diet *and* to eat, the latter – possibly understandably – has been neglected in social theory addressing anorexia, together with the economic forces underlying it. It is argued that food systems theory has an important part to play in explaining not only the compulsion to eat and to diet, but why the two are both compatible, if contradictory. There are also methodological parallels to be drawn from the study of eating disorders. For they can be understood as the specific and complex outcome of underlying tensions (to eat and to diet) that are social, and not purely individual, in origin and that are common to us all, with the possibility of a variety of outcomes – whether these be considered pathological (as in anorexia, bulimia and obesity) or not (as in the diet syndrome and the weight dissatisfaction particularly associated with women).

Chapter 4 critically examines the literature on what is termed the 'food information system'. This literature has primarily been oriented around what is perceived to be the practical, policy goal of shifting consumers' beliefs and, consequently, their purchasing behaviour and diet. Such an approach is shown to provide an erroneous analytical starting point on two closely related but distinct scores. First, the notion of knowledge, information or beliefs that is employed is seriously inadequate both in its scope and in the failure to recognise how ideas about food are generated, employed and frequently subject to inconsistency and fluidity. The creation of food beliefs needs to be related to a food information system that includes health messages and other sources of knowledge such as advertising, but which is fundamentally dependent upon the functioning of the food system itself as a source of practical knowledge – not least in how we cook, shop and eat. Second, not surprisingly, the impact of healthy eating advice has to be understood in the context of the functioning of the food system as a whole, and not merely at the proximate determinants of food choice alone. Indeed, in parallel with the suggestion for the formation of a food studies discipline, it is possible to organise the food information literature according to how it recognises, or contributes to the understanding of, food systems, the food information system and the interaction between the two.

Chapter 5 is more closely concerned with food policy. Standard analysis of the impact of the European Union's Common Agricultural Policy (CAP) on what we eat has suggested that it is small if costly since prices are higher without altering demand that much. This approach is criticised for neglecting the position of the CAP in the structure and functioning of the food systems as a whole, reducing it to a simple shift in supply.

Further, given emphasis upon the role of the food system as a whole in determining what we eat, it is hardly surprising that it is argued that food policy must address each component of the food system and not just the immediate determinants of food choice by the consumer. In this way, it proves possible to uncover how policy interventions might be neutralised or even reinforced by the operation of the food system. To this end, Chapter 5 also assesses the experience of Norwegian food policy, which has often been recognised as uniquely seeking to coordinate interventions to promote healthy eating with agricultural policy. Whilst rightly praised for attempting to merge two policy areas that are usually separately formulated and implemented and inconsistent with one another, initial optimism about the impact of such policy compatibility has given way to disillusion. This is shown to be the result of insufficient commitment to exercise control over the imperatives of the food system and the economic and political interests to which they are attached.

The final chapter offers a short but sharply critical appraisal of current proposals to establish a Food Standards Agency in the UK. Whilst universally welcomed for removing policy from the Ministry of Agriculture, Fisheries and Food (MAFF) and placing it under an independent, single and open authority, the proposals are shown to be severely deficient for responding primarily to issues of health and safety rather than those of nutrition and diet, for failing to recognise the need to coordinate food and agricultural policy with health as first priority, and for unduly continuing to rely upon trickle-down models of knowledge as far as the determinants of food choice are concerned.

2

RESOLVING THE DIET
PARADOX

Introduction

Just as the study of consumption has increasingly come to the fore analytically over the past two decades, so has the study of food consumption. Despite frequent claims of neglect, it has been far from starved. The references in the survey of Mennell *et al.* (1992) run to well over 500 items. To this must be added the well-established disciplines around agrarian studies, marketing, psychology and, at the immediate policy level, health and nutrition. Economists and historians have long been concerned with food supply and demand. There is no shortage of academic literature and, within the more popular media, there is no end to discussion of dieting and cooking. A number of developments, some theoretical and some empirical, have pushed food studies into even greater prominence. Consumption in general has been elevated within the confines of postmodernism to the forefront of contemporary social theory. Concern with the environment, the quality of food and the diseases of affluence have been important in promoting food as an object both of popular concern and, increasingly, of scholarship.

The purpose of this chapter is to take one pace back from the literature, to investigate what might give food studies one or more unifying themes. This is not motivated as an empirical exercise in the sociology of knowledge – yielding a frequency distribution of explanatory variables across the literature. Rather the purpose is to propose that certain themes are essential if food studies is to constitute an academic field that is coherent and integral but also distinctive from other areas, especially if food is to be set apart from other items of consumption.

This is an appropriate task and one that is more neglected than the study of food itself. For, often these studies have merely served as the means to apply a previously developed hypothesis. Thus, if your social theory concerns stratification, ritual, socialisation or whatever, so your application to consumption will attempt to test whether, or illustrate the way in which, the world of goods bears out the underlying analysis in practice. As Mennell *et al.* (1992) have observed of food, there has been a sociology of food but it has been more concerned with sociology than with food as such. This raises the problem of how social theory in general should confront particular items of consumption, even broad categories such as food. As observed, much of the previous literature does not even broach the issue.

To put it bluntly, what distinguishes food from other items of consumption as far as its determinants and significance are concerned? Does it trace out a clearly demarcated terrain of investigation? On the face of it, the answer would appear to be in the affirmative. Along with the growing interest in consumption, there has been an expanding range of studies dealing with food. But can they claim to constitute a well-defined academic field? If they are merely the raw material for applying theories that have nothing as such to do with food, then they simply make up a disparate set of empirical and theoretical case studies, any one of which, in principle, has more resonance with a similar application to some other non-food item than it does to some other food. In short, the whole would appear to be less than the sum of the individual parts. Hence, there is no apparent unifying theme in Mennell *et al.* (1992), merely a range of categories within which food has been examined, each of which is made up of a number of separate elements. There is no impression of food studies as an integral whole.[1]

Consider, for example, a popular starting point for food studies, the dictum 'You are what you eat'.[2] It has given birth to a wealth of studies that, from a variety of perspectives, establish a link between food and identity, whether this be individual or social. But similar exercises could be paraded for consumption as a whole or for other specific items of 'Tell me what you consume . . . ' or 'Tell me where you live, or what car you drive, or how you decorate your house, or what clothes you wear, . . . '.[3] Each of these has the same level of plausibility, and food is not distinctive by this criterion of being able to distinguish between consumers. Possibly, it could be argued that food is able to do this better than other items of consumption, but this has not been demonstrated. It does not even appear to have been recognised as a worthwhile exercise.[4]

Indeed, ironically, where food is used to serve as an index of distinction, it does so in a way that does not set it apart. If a food is perceived to be consumed as an act of differentiation or emulation, for example, then it (as well as the consumer) is distinguished from other foods that do not function in this fashion and is not distinguished from non-food items, other than in name, that also function in the same way. What has been characteristic of food studies, then, is that whilst their domain has been extended enormously, they have been equally heterogeneous in analytical content, in ways that do not specifically mark out food. The simplest way to see this is in terms of the presumed correspondence between the physical attributes of foods and their contribution to self-identity or lifestyle – chocolates are sweet, meat is strong, and so on. By this route, it would be possible to make a list of a hundred or more variables that have been used to explain the consumption of food and its meaning. In parallel with the use of food as a raw material for a more general social theory, the use of these variables is not specific to food. Thus, Douglas and Gross (1981) point to the wide range of variation and intricacy with which food functions socially and pursue this *by analogy* with clothing.[5] In this respect, then, food and clothing serve the same social and analytical purposes. *Neither* is distinctive, even though one is worn on the body and one ingested within it.

In short, there is a paradox to be found within the emerging discipline of food studies. On the one hand, whilst the range of analyses on what we eat has broadened, providing the rationale for a new academic field, it has only done so by undermining the notion that there is something integral about food. The various approaches to food have been fragmented and heterogeneous, defying an overall coherence. Farb and Arpelagos (1983) refer to a massive variety of examples in the anthropology of eating, and categorise these according to techno-environmental factors, social structure and ideology. Grivetti *et al.* (1987) consider that the culture of nutrition tangles a Gordian knot of factors. Richardson (1990) lists twelve broad psychological functions relevant to the acceptance of new foods. The magnitude of theories and of explanatory variables is not just an accidental misfortune, but follows from the frequent failure to distinguish the specificity of food as an item of consumption. Nonetheless, on the other hand, implicitly or otherwise, the idea persists that there is something integral about food consumption as a whole, to which particular studies can make their contribution. In other words, the study of food tends to presume the existence of a general underlying framework of analysis or object of study even as this is essentially negated in practice through the cumulative scholarship around food.

This situation will be termed the 'diet paradox' – to reflect the notion that there is an overall diet that can be the object of food studies and, yet, the fact that it proves analytically elusive. Is food special as an item of consumption or not? And if it is special, in what way is it set apart from other consumables? The literature, taken as a whole, has been careless with these questions. Hence the paradox is one of creating a field of food studies in name but not in analytical coherence. Food studies only develops by undermining itself!

The choice of the term 'diet paradox' is attractive for a number of reasons, other than in addressing the coherence of food studies as a discipline. First, there is the ambiguity, even self-contradiction, in the meaning of 'diet' itself. On the one hand, it means what we eat. It has also come, paradoxically, to mean not eating or restraining from eating. Second, diet suggests purposeful human behaviour. Animals feed. They do not or are not considered to have a diet – except in rare circumstances, usually attached to a single creature, often a pet, where anthropomorphism is involved. Third, one aspect of this second feature is that diet suggests choice as the form taken by purposeful behaviour. Yet diet is itself often conceived of in terms of the physical content of what is eaten. Indeed, much of the research on diet attempts to treat it as if it were the consequence of animal behaviour, as in serving physiological needs, and, where it is not, it seeks to link diet to other automatic mechanisms, such as emotions or broader psychological factors, that are a token symbol acknowledging the distinction between humans and animals. Fourth, a further aspect of the second feature is that diet applies both to the individual and to society more broadly; for the latter, as in the notion that there are national, Mediterranean, working-class and Asian diets, and so on.

Finally, though, the chief factor which prompted, if not justified, the notion of a diet paradox is derived from Fischler's (1989) use of the term in his notion of the omnivore's paradox. For him, the human consumption of food is caught between the tension of being able to eat anything in principle and bearing the risk of doing so in practice. As will be seen, such an insight is itself questionable if interpreted as intensifying under the conditions of contemporary capitalism, is not specific to food as such, and does not form the basis for establishing food studies as a comprehensive and coherent discipline.

Many of these tensions in the meaning of diet will be taken up elsewhere in this book. But how is the diet paradox to be resolved? Two previously developed propositions will suffice.[6] First, in general, it is possible to provide a theoretical framework to distinguish one consumption food, or broad category of consumption, from another through systems of provision. On that basis, the second step is to specify what is peculiar to the determinants of food consumption in particular – namely, the importance of the organic properties of food throughout the system of provision.

In short, what distinguishes one item of consumption from another is the system of provision to which each is attached. The separate components of the system of provision have to be situated relative to one another in order to pinpoint their role and significance. Further, the food system is not only set apart from others as a system but is uniquely dependent throughout upon an organic content. Thus, food studies can be defined as the analysis, conscious or otherwise, of (the components of) the food system. Contributions to the discipline are stronger the more they are integrated, or capable of integration, into an analysis of the food system whilst acknowledging its organic content.

Throughout this introduction, it has been presumed that it is appropriate to set our sights on the target of an integral discipline of food studies. This requires some justification but, first, some clarification. What is not intended is that academic departments of food studies should be encouraged to spring up everywhere, although such developments are not precluded, alongside those of the more traditional disciplines. Rather, the rationale for constituting food studies as an integral discipline lies in the analytical imperatives that it involves. For, as is consistently argued throughout the book, the different factors influencing the consumption and significance of food need to be situated in relationship to one another, and attached to the systems of provision for particular foods. The point is that the separate elements that make up the world of food need to be related to one another in order that, even in isolation from one another, the significance of each can be fully and properly understood and situated. In analytical, empirical and policy work, the examples of free-floating contributions to food studies are as numerous as they are not so much erroneous as misleading. Ultimately, however, the case for an integral food studies rests on the proof of the pudding being in the eating. The worth of resolving the diet paradox in the way suggested here rests on results in this and the previous volume (Fine *et al.*, 1996).

17

It also rests on taking existing literature as a critical point of departure. In what follows, the above conclusions are illustrated by a highly selective dip into the food studies literature. It begins with a discussion around one extreme in which, at the expense of other considerations, the organic significance of food tends to be focused upon as an exclusive preoccupation, as in nutritional studies. The latter discipline is marked by the notion of diet as a set of, and target for, nutrients as a result of their organic properties for human consumption. Other contributions to food studies, as will be shown, have also proceeded by focusing upon the organic properties of food in other ways, in relating to sociocultural factors, as in health or other food beliefs. In each case, the substance of what is contributed analytically is limited by the failure to consider the specific foods and the other factors attached to their provision.

The discussion of nutritional studies and other organically based literature is followed by an account of a putative contribution to food studies at the opposite extreme to that based on the organic content of food. For the organic content of food is notable only by its absence – in mainstream economic analysis as in appeal to Engel's Law and the notion that food expenditure follows systematic patterns on the basis of given preferences in response to shifting prices and incomes. It is remarkable that the economics of food should be reduced to so few explanatory factors, a consequence of the narrowness of the analysis and its failure to address the specifics of food.

The organic content of food

As an example of an explicit attention to the organic content of food, consider the approach to diet to be found in nutritional studies. Here, the organising idea is that there is a balanced diet or a composite bundle of nutrients which should be part and parcel of any individual's food consumption. And the object of policy is to guarantee or to persuade consumers to conform to dietary guidelines. Of course, it is recognised that different individuals have different requirements, and also that there is considerable variation in eating habits and deviation from guidelines. There is also recognition that there are a multitude of motives and material factors other than nutritional sustenance that determine diet. Yet the idea persists that there is some 'normal', physiologically determined standard of consumption around which eating behaviour should be understood, even if by way of deviance. As it were, the question is posed of why individuals do or do not consume the appropriate diet, and their eating and drinking behaviour is understood in these terms. Whilst this is understandable, given the policy goal of closing the gap between actual and recommended dietary intake, it is far from satisfactory as an analytical starting point. Indeed, as studies of food consumption tend to show, so heterogeneous are the determinants of diet that eating behaviour is not organised around individual knowledge and targets of healthy norms to be attained. And even where it is, these are liable to be imperfectly understood and imperfectly carried out in practice. Thus, the nutritional approach to food consumption employs some sort of dietary norms as an organising principle, but these are entirely analytically inappropriate for causal purposes.

Indeed, once attention turns to what causes the deviations, then these factors turn out to be more important in determining what is eaten than the physiologically determined norms from which they are considered to cause a departure. It is simply an artificial procedure to start with an 'ideal' diet and explain why it is not adopted. It seems more appropriate to explain directly what is eaten. Consider, for example, that a favoured starting point for explaining poor nutrition is often perceived to be the consequence of poor dietary information, suggesting remedies in terms of healthy eating campaigns. But, as argued in Chapter 4, knowledge about food and its influence upon eating habits is far more varied and complex; it is heavily derived from the experiences associated with obtaining, preparing and eating food. The informational determinants of food choice need to be set within an understanding of the food system itself, all sources of knowledge (termed the food information system) and their interaction. In short, an ideal diet and its promotion play only a minor and mediated role in determining overall food choice as well as in the selection of individual items.

Even setting aside the issue of food knowledge (and, further, its relation to the cultural significance of food), much of the literature has demonstrated that a major obstacle to healthy eating is to be found in the price of food, access to it in terms of shopping, time and technology available for preparation, competing demands from within the household according to its composition, and so on. Once again, taking these factors into consideration suggests that, as part of the food system, they are the proximate determinants of food choice, not the source of deviation from a nutritional norm.

Of course, the case for analysis around a nutritional standard appears to be stronger where deficient diets are associated with bare survival and where the apparent room for flexibility in consumption is circumscribed by limited resources. As Burghardt (1990, p. 307) succinctly puts it, 'the human body is taken to be a more or less standard item of equipment as indicated by the so-called *Recommended Daily Allowance* that continues to inform so much research on nutritional deficiency'.[7] However this is determined, nourishment is identified with 'real' food, something that is as much socially constructed within the poorest societies as it is in those societies or for those consumers where the absolute availability of food is not at issue. Thus, pregnant and nursing mothers are subject to culturally determined diets, interacting with other material factors.[8] And the availability of food is determined by the complex processes associated with the food system. Thus, Harriss (1990) rejects simplistic models of malnutrition (and its relation to health) even when based upon some notion of intra-household power at the expense of females. She concludes that factors other than patriarchy are at work, including social class, age, technology, skills, inheritance practices, and so on.[9]

Clearly, because of the focus on nutritional requirements, there is within nutritional studies a definite connection to the specificity of food – in contrast to those approaches which project a general social theory onto food. Diet is linked to physiological needs, to the organic content of food necessary to sustain the healthy body. The virtue of nutrition-based studies is that they do recognise, at the point of consumption, a necessary feature which, in part, sets food aside from other items of consumption. But there are arguably greater weaknesses. First, other items of consumption have an organic content in product or in their use – clothes and medicine, respectively, for example. So organic content as such is not sufficient to set food aside from all other items of consumption unless, as argued previously, this feature is recognised along the system of provision as a whole. Second, as indicated by the few examples considered, once diet is interrogated analytically, it is found to have only the loosest connection to its organic content, and a range of other material and cultural factors have to be brought in to play, however much they extend along the food system. The organic is important but it is far from being the determining factor in diet, even by way of deviance. It has nothing to commend it as an analytical starting point for understanding diet.

As such it might be termed a primitive approach to diet. This is not because of its lack of sophistication, for the physiological and biochemical knowledge necessary to construct an ideal diet, and the effects of deviating from it, lie far beyond the capabilities of the present author. Rather, it is primitive because it treats the human diet on a par with the feeding behaviour of an extremely clever if, at times, capricious animal. This is even true as analysis steps outside nutritional studies to broader psychological, economic and other factors. For these, respectively, are often understood as little more than the learning and instinctive behaviour of a particular species, and the extent of feeding availability through the market.

There are surely few who continue to believe that the nutritional content of food determines what is consumed, even if the idea persists that other factors lead to divergence from appropriate norms.[10] A similar analytical structure can be found, with the organic married to the social, through a norm determined other than by nutritional content. Consider, for example, the so-called 'omnivore's paradox', for which there is a tension between the potential to incorporate a wider variety of foods within diet and the dangers associated with the consumption of the new or unknown. This is a source of anxiety and arises because of the omnivore's ability to eat most things but with uncertain biological effects (Fischler, 1980, 1988, 1989). A similar, if more broadly cast, argument is to be found in the notion of the 'delocalisation' of food provision (Pelto and Pelto, 1985; Pelto and Vargas, 1992). Commercialisation of food, and access to it by consumers through the market from distant and unknown methods of production, means that local knowledge of food is undermined. Consequently, both the material and cultural components of the food systems need to be assessed.

There are, however, serious problems with this approach, especially in the form taken by Fischler's account, despite its organic content. It is as if the consumer is stranded on an exotic desert island, faced with a choice of unfamiliar berries, potentially nutritious or poisonous. It must be questioned how relevant such considerations are to contemporary, or even earlier, consumption decisions. Accordingly, Fischler (1989) argues that the paradox persists but has been displaced along, and concealed within, the modern food system. Consumers no longer have direct choices to make over the content of their food, which can serve as a means of expressing identity and of social incorporation. Anxiety is intensified by the conflicts over the cultural content of food, especially as the modern eater has become a mere consumer, removed from knowledge of the origins and content of food, increasingly individualised and stripped of a social culinary system, and subject to food panics and crises of self-identity. It must also be recognised, however, that the same 'progress' that commercialises food also brings us *greater* knowledge about it in a whole variety of ways, even if this is a different knowledge than that associated with a more primitive form of production, more intimately and directly attached to consumption. The material and cultural construction of food, and food knowledge, become different in content and composition.[11] It is not clear that the best way to understand these is either through a persisting omnivore's paradox or through a delocalisation of food.

Within this sort of approach, then, the organic content of food can be socially projected onto what you are, and how you experience – as being animal- or vegetable-like, for example. For Rozin (1990), food thereby takes on moral attributes, subject to associations with contagion and disgust, reflecting a conflation of the physical and the socially constructed properties of foods. A similar stance is adopted by Fiddes (1991), who sees the eating of meat as symbolic of command over nature, something which loses its appeal in the twentieth century, thereby inducing vegetarianism.[12] For van den Berghe (1984, p. 388):

> We evolved into a terrestrial, bipedal, diurnal, omnivorous,
> food gatherer and hunter, forming relatively stable,
> longlasting pair bonds between adult males and females
> cooperating in the nurturance of their highly dependent
> offspring through a domestic economy based on a sexual
> division of labour and food exchange.

He sees these evolutionary characteristics as creating the basis for socialisation, behavioural reinforcement and, ultimately, ethnicity in food consumption as a means of demarcating frontiers between communities.

Each of these positions might also be described as primitive, even if in a different way than in nutritional studies. For the common logic of each is an organic essentialism in which historically previous tensions around diet in earlier forms of social reproduction are projected onto the present in the form of continuing conflicts. An organically based tension, conflict or paradox is identified, however accurately, for an earlier, more 'primitive' stage of food consumption; this is then presumed to be deeply embedded in the more complex forms of organisation and meanings associated with the modern food systems. There is a striking parallel with nutritional norms as an essential core around which behaviour is organised; only now it is the human condition, motivations and uncertainties. Similarly, though, it must be doubted whether it is appropriate to take such socially constructed behavioural norms as an analytical starting point. Indeed, Jerome (1975), without reference to the organic nature of food, is able to observe the tension between expanding variety of foods and accepting a core diet in the context of the individualised consumer confronting the modern US supermarket – which flavour of ice-cream, crisps or whatever; the anxiety of choice does not have to be based upon organic uncertainties.

A further significant example of literature within food studies that recognises its organic content are those works that address the relationship between food and health.[13] The most obvious connection is that both food and medicines tend to be taken by mouth. In addition, whilst medicines are intended to cure, there is a often a strong association presumed between diet and health, not just amongst nutritionists but also in the cultural interpretations of and, hence, the rationale for consuming foods. So common has this become that health movements are often associated with particular diets and, thereby, dubbed as incorporating a fad (this even being used to denigrate any concern with diet).[14] Calnan and Williams (1991, p. 521) find that 'health concerns were expressed spontaneously almost exclusively in relation to food', with corresponding attempts to change diet. This may reflect a fatalism about disease in other areas[15] (other than smoking, drinking and hygiene, which may have been taken for granted). Whilst foods that generate disgust or taboo may, in fact, be harmless, there is often an association with health in so far as foods are interpreted (rightly or wrongly) as being hygienic or safe in ways that are profoundly influenced by cultural factors. In this respect, Foster and Kaferstein (1985) are able to list almost thirty sociocultural factors that influence diet through their impact on beliefs about food safety. This reinforces the conclusion that opening up the diet paradox, in this case through the relationship between food and health, requires both the food system and the organic properties of food to be examined in conjunction with one another.

The organic content of food is also recognised in dieting – clearly an increasingly important aspect of food choice, one associated with lifestyle by Leachwood (1990); food is partly perceived to affect health but, more crucially, shape.[16] Thus, in explaining medical conditions such as bulimia and anorexia nervosa, it is insufficient to point to the intense psychological stresses associated with the most susceptible group, young women. It is also necessary to explain why these stresses should take food-related forms rather than present themselves as other symptoms of obsession. Chernin (1986), for example, suggests that young women may be resisting the change in bodily shape associated with physical maturity and that mother-rejection may be reflected in food as weaning is an early and deep-rooted form of rejection which has an immediate connection with feeding. However, whatever the psychological pressures to consume or not, account must surely also be taken of the availability of food and the commercial pressures exerted by the food system in generating demand for its products and the benefits that they bestow upon the consumer. It seems quite remarkable that the rising incidence of eating disorders should be so readily associated with the psychological pressures of contemporary society (women to be slim for men but also independent of them, for example) but with little or no account taken of the imperatives to consume that derive from those who profit from food.[17]

Does Engel's Law really apply to food?

In the previous section, reference has been made to some of the literature that incorporates an organic component into its under-standing of food. An economist's approach to the integral nature of diet is very different. Analysis of food as an item of consumption has been organised around Engel's Law, a presumed regularity between income and the composition of expenditure – as income rises the proportion spent on food declines.[18] Since the formulation of the hypothesis in the middle of the nineteenth century, further work has taken two inter-related directions.[19] First, there has been theo-retical investigation of the conditions under which the hypothesis does or does not hold true. Second, this has been subject to econo-metric testing. This has involved a series of problems within the traditional confines of orthodox neoclassical economics.[20] These concern separability of utility, aggregation conditions (over house-holds and over sub-sample populations with different socioeconomic characteristics), corner solutions (not all commodities might be purchased), dynamic specifications (consumption decisions take place over time), and the interaction between labour market outcomes and consumption and saving decisions.

It is important to emphasise that this literature does not question what constitutes a diet. It presumes that there is a well-defined category of food and then investigates whether this satisfies conditions associated with Engel's Law. The organic nature of food does not figure, unless it is implicit that there is a limited capacity to the stomach. This can then only accommodate so much expenditure, a decreasing proportion as income rises. Yet more expenditure is absorbed with income, although partly as a consequence of increasing quality and, therefore, unit price. If Engel's Law does hold, the implication is that quality of food is also sufficiently income-inelastic. But there would appear to be no capacity constraints for quality.

Such simple considerations reinforce the observation that Engel's Law, whether confirmed or not, is simply a rough-and-ready empirical account of expenditure on food with little conceptual care taken over how food is understood. That this is so is brought out by sampling some of the literature. Lahiri (1990), for example, argues that it is necessary to disaggregate by foods, as some satisfy Engel's Law and others do not, a result for meats found by Ryan *et al.* (1982); Karagiannis and Velentzas (1997) find that demand for foods reflects habit formation but that the effect is heterogeneous across different foods. Thus, foods would not appear to form an integral whole for the purposes of investigating income elasticities.[21] Jackson (1984) suggests that utility is satisfied through a hierarchy of wants, so that the range of commodities purchased (as well as the quantities) varies with income. Thus, the causes of switching from one product to another are of importance in determining what foods are consumed as well as their quantities. Most interesting is the contribution of Stigler and Becker (1977), for it seeks to show how as many as possible of the apparent anomalies associated with demand theory can be explained on the basis of given, even common, preferences (rather than the more usual procedure of relying upon changes in preference as a residual explanatory factor).[22] Thus, it is recognised that consumption is distinct from purchase as the household can itself produce on the basis of commodity inputs. If there is a shift in comparative advantage between household and commercial production, then expenditure on foods will not correctly track the proportion of resources devoted to them. It is also argued that consumption may not be addictive or habit-forming as such but may appear so given a rational, optimising decision to gain from the cumulative experience of (producing for) consumption. As it were, there is learning-by-consuming in which preferences remain the same but consumption human-capital is accrued over time (like learning-by-doing within work and the accumulation of human capital through work-experience). This explains what are presumed to be the more sophisticated tastes of wealthier and more elderly consumers. Finally, advertising is not perceived as manipulating demand curves through influencing preferences but as providing a joint product – of the commodity itself, as well as of information about it (a contribution to consumption human-capital) for which an extra price has to be paid.[23]

The purpose here is less to assess the validity of such ingenious analytical acrobatics as to point out how the determinants of food consumption, even within this narrow and abstract framework, are broadened beyond immediate proximate factors (price, income and utility) to incorporate advertising, habit formation, domestic production, and so on. Further, the inference drawn by Engel from his observation of declining share of expenditure on food was that this would entail a corresponding decline in the share of national income accounted for by agriculture. With increasing productivity within this sector, there is a need for resources to shift out of it. This gives rise to the farm problem in terms of those who have to make the adjustment and the depressed terms under which they have to do it – if adjustment is not fast enough, it leads to excess supply and relatively low rural incomes.[24] This suggests that Engel's Law itself is liable to depend upon the relative productivity of agriculture.[25] In short, the determinants of food consumption are varied and need to be traced back to their origins in production.

It is worth recalling that this conclusion is reached despite taking preferences and the nature of food as given – unreasonable assumptions within most other social sciences. It is a consequence of looking upon the economy as a (general equilibrium) system in which supplies and demands mutually condition one another and simultaneously determine all prices and outputs. Goods destined for final consumption embody a multiplicity of utility-enhancing characteristics,[26] much like the nutritional approach to food but with a wider range of potential benefits. Whatever the merits of such analysis as economic theory, its failure to confront the organic nature of food means that diet (expenditure on food) forms an integral whole (subject or not to Engel's Law) only as the outcome of statistical investigation, contingent upon how food is defined. Significantly, Engel curves can equally be investigated for other commodity groups, such as housing, clothing, transport and leisure.[27] It might be thought that, subject to quality, there are limited capacities to consume. Consider, however the interdependence between these categories. Expenditure on food can increase with income if it is associated with offering hospitality (a form of leisure); it may not be subject to capacity constraints if its waste is a means of signalling affluence; and eating out involves transport, dressing-up, and so on. Should these be included as expenditure on food? On the other hand, consumer durables may allow savings to be made in expenditure on food: do cooking utensils constitute expenditure on food or not? They would do so if the food was brought pre-prepared with the wear and tear of utensils (even if passed on from large-scale machinery) included in the price.

Concluding remarks

As previously suggested, the conundrum of defining food as an object of study is most usefully addressed by incorporating an organic component into an analysis based on distinct systems of provision. Discussion around Engel's Law ultimately departs from this by failing to specify what food is (organically and socially) and by allowing all production and consumption to contribute to given insatiable utility in the same way, whether directly or indirectly, and therefore without distinction between systems of provision. Nutritional studies lie at the opposite extreme, emphasising the organic content of food and whether or not choice is distorted away from a balanced diet. It would appear that the only means by which these two approaches could be reasonably integrated is through the method suggested here. Further, it is possible to organise and categorise the literature around food according to the way in which it addresses one or more components of the food system, and the extent to which it incorporates an organic component. Hopefully, the few examples considered here illustrate that this is a worthwhile exercise for others to pursue as well as a contribution towards establishing food studies as a well-defined discipline drawn across the social sciences.

3

THE POLITICAL ECONOMY OF EATING DISORDERS

As Durkheim argues, greater powers and capacities, a greater range of activity, mean that the individual can experience a wider variety of pleasures and perhaps it may heighten their intensity. By the same token, however, it also increases the range and intensity of the pain and discomfort experienced.

(Sayers, 1994, pp. 72–3)

Introduction

Given access to sufficient food, classifications of ill-health arising out of eating problems usually fall into three categories with corresponding literatures, academic disciplines, medical treatments, and policy proposals that rarely intersect with one another. The categories are food contamination, the eating diseases of western affluence, and eating disorders. The first is distinguished by perceiving the consumer as unwitting victim of the failure to provide food hygienically as a result of contamination, broadly interpreted, although the consumer is potentially responsible for failing to preserve and prepare food appropriately. The policy response is to regulate conditions governing the safety of food, to educate the consumer in the acquisition and preparation of food prior to consumption, to treat individual cases of ill-health, and to handle food scares as and when they arise.[1]

The second category denotes unwise choice in the composition and quantity of food, usually resulting in long-term ill-health as a consequence of poor diet. Policy here primarily focuses upon discovering and treating the causes of diseases such as coronary heart disease and inculcating a healthier diet through making more nutritional information available and inducing consumers to absorb and act upon it. Between these two categories, there is an overlap in the use of information as a source of change, with a hint of blaming the victim for lacking or not acting upon different types of knowledge, and with the first category placing much greater emphasis upon regulation and the second upon education. Each rests upon some sort of notion of food knowledge and education, as well as different aspects of the science of food and nutrition, although each of these components can be addressed in isolation from one another. The same applies to the way in which the food system moulds itself around these aspects of the ill-health attached to food and responds to policy initiatives. Is regulation of health and safety effective, for example, and with what effects? On the other hand, is the consumer well informed and basing consumption on an appropriate under-standing of food health and safety?

The third category, eating disorders, is distinguished from the others by the presumption of a sufficiently severe disjuncture in the functioning of the consumer to warrant diagnosis of a mental disorder. This is most sharp in the case of anorexia, or self-starvation, slightly less so for bulimia (alternating starving and/or purging and excessive eating), and least severe for obesity, where the physical symptoms might not in and of themselves be taken to be indicative of mental disorder requiring psychiatric care. For eating disorders, the focus is upon the individual who is no longer held as responsible for outcomes in a simple way. The consumer becomes a patient and is judged not to be adequately capable in mental health. Analytical focus is primarily from within the discipline of psychology, treatment from psychiatry, and policy response is notable for its absence. You do not regulate or educate consumers not to suffer from eating disorders any more than offering leaflets informing the public on how not to be insane! The understanding and treatment of eating disorders is based upon the consumer being treated as being both medically and mentally ill.

This chapter is concerned with eating disorders, some of the other issues being taken up in other chapters. This is not intended to imply an acceptance of the traditional distinction between the categories of eating problems outlined above. Even if there were clear boundaries between them empirically, it is readily shown that the problems share certain causal factors in common which, in addi-tion, are experienced by all consumers, even if in less extreme forms or with less extreme results.

Consider, for example, the problem of obesity. In the United States, it is estimated that 31 per cent of men and 24 per cent of women are overweight, with a body-mass index (BMI) of over 25 – the healthy level adjudged to be in the low twenties.[2] Approximately 12 per cent of both men and women are severely overweight with BMI in excess of 30 per cent (Brownell and Rodin, 1994).[3] Comparable figures for the UK for BMI greater than 30 are 13 per cent for men and 15 per cent for women in 1991, compared to 7 per cent and 12 per cent, respectively, just five years earlier (Coles and Turner, 1995). As the population has become more overweight, the preoccupation with, and practice of, dieting has reached epidemic proportions with limited, even perverse, impact upon weight. Between 1950 and 1966, 7 per cent of men and 14 per cent of women in the United States were attempting to lose weight. This had risen to 24 per cent and 40 per cent, respectively, by 1993, with 37 per cent of men and 52 per cent of women considering themselves to be overweight (Brownell and Rodin, 1994). Robison et al. (1993) reckon that 20 per cent of schoolchildren in the US are dieting to lose weight. Biener and Heaton (1995) report that 64 per cent of women and 23 per cent of men have been on diets in the past even though they have never been overweight.[4] At the same time that treatment of obesity is reckoned to incur a cost of $40 billion per year, 5.5 per cent of health care expenditure (Brownell and Wadden, 1992),[5] the dieting industry has a turnover in excess of $20 billion (Rothblum, 1992).[6] For the UK, West (1994) puts the direct cost of obesity to the National Health Service at £30 million, with indirect cost through the risk factor attached to other diseases at £165 million.[7] The paradoxical increasing incidence of dieting and obesity, and the limited effects of the former on weight of individuals even over relatively short periods of time, have led to a serious questioning of whether dieting is a suitable prescription for obesity.[8]

The extent of anorexia and bulimia are less dramatic than for obesity and dieting as such. The balance between females and males is reckoned at about ten to one, but the balance is shifting, and both conditions appear to be becoming more common, but with bulimia only emerging to prominence from the 1970s onwards with what appear to be cohort effects (Russell, 1995; Szmukler and Patton, 1995).[9] This demonstrates that these eating disorders have a definite pattern, both increasing in incidence and changing in form, attracting those employing medical models to view them by analogy with conventional diseases which spread (contagion but through a copy-cat effect) and evolve (from anorexia to bulimia).[10]

Even from this initial, cursory overview, it is apparent that eating disorders are of considerable significance in terms of their economic and social effects, quite apart from the severity of ill-health and unhappiness with which they are associated. It also transpires that we inhabit a very peculiar world in which dieting and overeating co-exist and prosper together. When these activities take on extreme forms and give rise to eating disorders, it is time to call the doctor or, more exactly, the psychiatrist or therapist. Whether effective at the level of individual treatment or not, it is argued in the next section that it is appropriate to move beyond the focus upon the individual and to examine the social, cultural as well as the economic factors underlying eating disorders. This implies, as argued in the following section, that eating disorders should be understood not simply as a disorder of the individual psyche but as the particular forms assumed by the socially generated pressures both to eat and to diet.

The remainder of this chapter is concerned to establish the economic basis for these pressures and why it is that both can intensify despite their apparent inconsistency. This involves asking why women should be particularly vulnerable to the pressures concerned, why thinness should have increasingly become the ideal norm for body image, and why food should, as it were, have become the object of stress management or dysfunction. The answers provided are disarmingly simple in suggesting that women have experienced an intensification of stress as they have sought to combine traditional beauty/mother roles with those of career and working, that the dieting industries have been able to complement rather than to compete with the food industries – by exaggerating the malleability of the body – despite its norm of slenderness. Moreover, food has become a direct focus for the stresses around eating and dieting as well as a target for other displaced stresses.

Why political economy?

The purpose of this section is to justify confronting eating disorders with the insights to be gained from political economy. This is an unusual coupling. For, although there has been a very rapid growth in literature concerned with eating disorders, the role of economic factors has been peripheral. As an initial, ground-clearing exercise, then, a start is made by justifying the confrontation between 'deviant' eating habits and economic analysis.

First, although it cannot reasonably be suggested that the individual incidence of eating disorders is the direct consequence of

31

economic factors, much the same could be said of vandalism and delinquency, for example. Yet it is considered appropriate to counterpose these with economic influences such as levels of unemployment and social deprivation. Turner (1987, p. 26) has pointed to the potential parallel between the sociology of crime and of sickness in general, with the latter needing to incorporate a political economy of health care. The case for linking economics with eating disorders is even stronger than for health issues as a whole because of the undoubted and heavy significance of social factors. Further, employing another example suggested by Turner, Durkheim analysed suicide as a topic within sociology in part to explain how suicide rates would vary without employing psychological factors pitched at the level of the individual. Although many eating disorders do lead to premature death, they do not involve a deliberate attempt at self-destruction any more than does smoking cigarettes. Nonetheless, it is demonstrably appropriate to incorporate social factors when addressing deviancy, disorder or whatever, whether this be in the context of crime, health or suicide.

Nor is the emphasis so far on social factors exclusive of economic considerations. For the evolution of (the recognition of) medical conditions and their treatment is a highly respectable and well-researched topic within economic and social history.[11] It has been found in retrospect that economic conditions are often more important than they were acknowledged to be at the time. It will be argued here that contemporary understanding of eating disorders has not overlooked economic factors but it has seriously neglected them. Here is an attempt to anticipate a future corrective to this neglect!

A second reason for addressing eating disorders from the perspective of political economy follows from the light that this sheds on deficiencies in the treatment of consumption within orthodox approaches, especially neoclassical economics.[12] For the latter, consumption is understood as the consequence of the demand derived from given preferences as income and prices change. Changes in preferences, though, are rarely examined but are exploited as the residual explanation for what cannot be explained statistically through prices and incomes on the basis of given preferences.[13] Eating disorders, individually, socially and historically, could be interpreted as indicating quite dramatic changes in preferences, thereby lying outside the realm of economics, if not political economy, since orthodox economics axiomatically takes preferences as both fixed and exogenously given. Elsewhere (Fine, 1995b,

1997b, 1998b), attempts by neoclassical economists such as Gary Becker to endogenise preferences have been criticised for perceiving deviancy in consumption, such as addiction, as the 'rational' strategic response to consumption possibilities over time. If the discounted future pain of 'learning' addiction is more than compensated for by the immediate pleasures of current consumption, then it is optimal for the individual to choose to become an addict. Such an approach to addiction (to eating or to dieting, for example) is sorely inadequate not only for the causal content that it offers, but also for the understanding itself of what it seeks to explain. Whether in eating disorders or consumption more generally as some form of addiction, the dramatic swings in behaviour and the stresses, motives and welfare attached to them are not indicative of individual, strategic optimisation in which future utility is sacrificed for the pleasures of the present. Thus, and the same applies to the treatment of consumption in disciplines other than orthodox economics, the analysis of eating disorders poses problems that stretch and undermine existing explanatory capacity and creates demands for a more sophisticated and complex explanatory framework.

Of course, where orthodox accounts of consumer behaviour break down, the response is to appeal to the irrationality of the preferences or actions concerned, thereby conveniently limiting the required scope of explanation to normal or rational behaviour which, more or less tautologously, is theoretically incorporated. Third, then, in justifying the application of political economy to eating disorders, it is particularly pertinent to examine the formation of potentially extreme food preferences – if not necessarily under this terminological guise. For it is now increasingly recognised that eating disorders represent conditions that are extreme responses to the pressures (for example, to thinness) that are experienced by most if not all women in contemporary capitalism. Consequently, unravelling the determinants of eating disorders does offer the promise of more general insights into the determinants of food and other types of consumption. Of course, it cannot always be argued that deviant or disordered behaviour is a route through which to arrive at a more general understanding of the issues involved in more moderate consumption. But a strong case can be made for this with regard to eating disorders. This is even so at the clinical stage of diagnosis where, for example, Russell (1995, p. 9) concludes a survey with the suggestion that 'anorexia nervosa is arguably but an extension of determined dieting'. Similarly, French *et al.* (1995, p. 700) conclude from their study of dieting adolescents[14] that

> Many have hypothesized eating disorders to be a qualitatively distinct phenomenon from chronic dieting . . . we believe that the present findings support the idea of a continuum of dieting behaviors . . . that dieting at subclinical levels is widespread in the general population of adolescent females and is associated with wide-ranging negative risk factors.

More generally, whether identifying the immediate symptoms of eating disorders (dieting, bingeing, purging, for example) or the closer or more distant causal factors in the pressures to eat and to diet (to be discussed later but including body image and control, for example), it is inevitably found that they are all experienced in common to a greater or lesser extent. In other words, if eating disorders are, and are caused by, society-wide characteristics which are shared in common, then unravelling them offers a fuller understanding of the economics of consumption.

In this light, anorexia is an eating disorder that can be interpreted as a dramatic response to the pressures experienced by *all* young women. It has led Orbach (1993) to view it as a 'Metaphor for our Time', one in which women have to accommodate their own needs and goals to the social expectations that are imposed upon them in conditions that are disadvantageous and obstructive. In the closing remarks of this chapter, however, anorexia will be exploited for a rather different metaphor, one of analytical method – to reflect upon our times rather than to reflect them. For eating disorders, as chronic or acute conditions, reveal how underlying pressures interact to give rise to such complex outcomes that they appear to defy both explanation and rationality. It is apparent that orthodox demand theory derived from economics is quite incapable of dealing with obsessive patterns of consumption since they violate the presumption of narrowly defined, rational behaviour. Indeed, bulimia nervosa, as alternating dependence upon binge and vomiting and often yielding normal body weight, would presumably be interpreted as a satisfactory net level of consumption arising out of a trade-off between the marginal utilities of eating and not eating. However, anorexia cannot be viewed as anything other than the outcome, rather than the resolution or balance, of extremely complex and powerful psychological pressures. Similarly, by way of metaphor or, more exactly, analytical method, the functioning of the food system can be interpreted as responding to the underlying economic forces that act upon it, rather than as the more or less harmonious interaction of supply and demand.

What are eating disorders?

As remarked in the previous section, eating disorders can be considered as representing forms of extreme behaviour along a continuum that includes all consumers. Broadly speaking, although finer classifications are possible, disorders are diagnosed as excessive and persistent dieting (as in anorexia), excessive eating (as in obesity) and some cyclical combination of the two (as in bulimia which, may be accompanied by vomiting and laxative abuse to purge the effects of bingeing).

Over the past decade, eating disorders have been the subject of intense attention. Almost three hundred academic articles a year have been devoted to the topic of anorexia and bulimia nervosa, with as many again if obesity is included.[15] These articles are, however, almost exclusively confined to the disciplines of psychology and psychiatry. This is all the more remarkable since it is uncontroversial that eating orders are social in origin, with specific historical, gender, class and geographical incidence. The origins of my own interest in eating disorders are significant. Asked to prepare a talk on the treatment of consumption in economic and social history, my use of the social science citation index around keywords such as consumption and gender yielded an overwhelming output of articles addressing deviancy in consumption, with food, smoking and alcohol to the fore. In extending my original work on food for this book, it was again found that the weight of the new social science literature on food is concerned with eating disorders.

One of the reasons for the slant in the academic literature is its origins in, and continuing attachment to, confrontation with, and treatment of, a medical condition. The result has been a focus upon the individual to be cured. In conformity to the notion of medicine as a natural science, research has sought to identify purely biological symptoms and mechanisms and to treat them accordingly. Essentially, the response is to take the symptoms at face value and to search for *internal* bodily functions, physical or mental, that are inducing disorderly eating habits or outcomes. From our perspective, even if this were appropriate and effective in individual cases, which is rare, it can shed no light upon why eating disorders should have arisen when and where they have.

Essentially, this deficiency is recognised in the extent to which the literature is concerned with *mental* disorder which may have *external* origins that are to be identified. Here, for example, there is a contrast with the study of those other eating diseases attached to western affluence, such as coronary heart disease and various cancers. Whilst these can reasonably be argued to have been caused by historically specific socioeconomic factors that have changed our diet and lifestyles, it is generally presumed that those who suffer the conditions are not mentally deranged in view of their choice of diet any more than a smoker is perceived at most to be unwise and short-sighted in endangering health.

Since those who suffer eating disorders are generally considered to have chosen their condition as opposed to those who suffer diseases from having smoken or eat badly, it is hardly surprising that the model of the sick inner body, whether mental or physical, should give way to a model of causes external to the body. Consequently, eating disorders are understood in terms of an individual pathology that ranges over socioeconomic status, family background, individual psychological history, and so on. There is, however, a crucial reason why eating disorders should engage psychiatrists and psychologists whereas smoking and a bad diet as a matter of course should not.[16] This is because of the high levels of stress that have been recognised to occur with eating disorders over and above the physical ill-health equally attached to coronary heart disease and the like. Taken together, what the literature highlights is the diversity and depth of stresses involved in eating disorders, and their increasing scale and scope over time – although this reflects, with the cumulative impact of more case studies and the shifting preoccupations of medicine itself, both the new discovery of associated stresses previously overlooked and the emergence of new stresses attached to eating.[17]

Currently, the stress around eating is heavily conditioned by the importance of body image, especially for women, and increasingly the notion that the body is itself malleable and subject to control. Initially, anorexia was associated with the wish of adolescent girls to impede their passage to sexual maturity. Fasting endowed them with a sense and, to an extent, the reality of control over their own bodies.[18] Today, the options for body control and body image are considerably expanded, reinforcing the notion of the potential for elasticity in bodyshape or, more exactly, body image.

The means for transforming body image are, even more than ever, no longer confined to eating habits. Contemporary capitalism offers us various forms of surgery, dieting and health products, fashion clothes, make-up, hairdressing and exercise.[19] These are all designed to alter (the appearance of) our bodies. It follows that, far from expanding the realm of freedom in shaping the contours of our bodies, we are caught up in the stresses of meeting social norms for our appearances and the stigma attached to failing to do so.

The extent of stress involved has been well documented in a number of ways. Ideal body image has become increasingly slender over the post-war period, as models and more general representation of women in the media have become thinner. Many women would prefer to lose weight than to achieve a whole range of what would normally be taken to be far more serious achievements in career and personal life. They are more liable to exercise for this purpose, especially relative to men, than for health as such, and a sense of self-esteem and self-control is closely associated with diet and weight, and guilt with eating.[20] In addition, body image by women is frequently misinterpreted in a variety of ways – with dieting even when weight is normal or healthy, and overestimation of size of own body image and underestimation of the ideals held by others. Perhaps most disturbing is the extent to which these associations between dieting and body image are prevalent even amongst girls of 9 years old or less, with boys less concerned for themselves at that age but, nonetheless, conscious and supportive of such norms for girls (Hill *et al.*, 1992; Thelen *et al.*, 1992).[21]

The pressures to mould the ideal body are demonstrated in the perfectionism associated with anorexics as well as the stigma attached to obesity. The overweight perceive themselves as failing to exercise self-control and, quite correctly, anticipate that perception in others.[22] Moreover, the stigma attached to obesity leads to discrimination against the obese – in job applications, for example.[23] So great is the stigma against the obese that Rothblum (1992) considers them to constitute an oppressed minority. Apart from discrimination, the obese are subject to the burden of five myths (Rothblum, 1990). These are that the definition of obesity is arbitrary, that it is particularly prevalent amongst women, that the obese eat more calories than the non-obese, that dieting is effective in reducing weight, and obesity is related to poor physical health.[24] Whilst these reservations need to be taken into account in recognising that obesity and its effects are socially constructed and subject to ambiguity and exaggeration, the extent and dangers of over-eating are well established.[25] In either case, the stresses around eating are pervasive.[26]

Nor are they moderated by the wider range of options that are available for moulding the malleable body. Rather, failure to achieve the ideal is even stronger evidence of lack of control over diet – not only do you eat too much, you exercise too little and neither clothes, make-up nor surgery is sufficient to compensate; hence, the pressure for the attractions of personality to compensate for deficiencies in physical shape. However, the increasing significance of body image as a source of stress is complemented by the wide and increasing range of the other associates of food and weight. Thus, anorexia is recognised as a compromise between achieving the goal of an ideal-shaped (thin) woman and the avoidance of 'maturity'.

The latter is most readily interpreted in sexual terms,[27] although it is complemented by the growing demands upon contemporary young women to be successful in education and career (a man's world, as it were) as well as to match traditional ideals of women as attractive to men, passive, and as wife and mother. In other words, if anorexia is understood as a refusal to become mature, so the content of what is being refused has expanded as the expectations of women have themselves become greater and potentially inconsistent.[28] Whatever its former role, sexual maturity may no longer be the key to what is being rejected along with food.[29] Nonetheless, most recently, in line with such concerns more widely, the attempt has been made to associate eating disorders with childhood trauma, particularly sexual abuse and varieties of sexual experience more generally.[30] Whilst some studies do find a connection, others discover that eating disorders are associated with a wide range of traumas, such as violence and other family dysfunction,[31] and that it is the greater susceptibility to deviancy in general in these circumstances that explains an apparent association with eating disorders.[32]

It is important, then, not to stereotype the symptoms associated with eating disorders. For anorexia, the literature has focused upon the trauma of female adolescence, associated with the rites of passage to adulthood (physical and independent control of the body, avoidance of sexuality, and yet the compulsion to be thin in order to be attractive), with a shifting relationship to other family members (particularly mother), and with the conflict between femininity and attainment, and so on.[33] However, Thompson (1992) questions existing explanatory models of anorexia by pointing to a multitude of traumas that have been associated with it – racism, sexual abuse, poverty, sexism, emotional or physical abuse, and heterosexism, for example.[34] Whatever the incidence of anorexia across those of different socioeconomic status, it is apparent that food can be the target of a number of displaced affects.

This is a consequence of the wide variety of meanings that can be attached to different foods for the population as a whole. As a result both of the wide variety of psychological symptoms associated with eating disorders and the generality, if not the extremity, of the emotions attached to them by all of us, it is hardly surprising that early diagnosis of anorexia proves difficult. Dieting and possibly comfort eating are commonplace amongst the majority of women to a greater or lesser extent, for example. More generally, as Butler (1988, p. 3) observes, there is an 'anorexic *state* . . . that collective experience shared by the majority of women in present-day Western society'. It is represented most sharply in the high profile of both slimming and cookery, symbolising women's dual role as both sex object and domestic labourer.

Stresses around food, then, can be divided into two sorts: those that are directly associated with food, as in body image; and those that are displaced onto food as in the avoidance of maturity and, not previously mentioned, the various emotional gratifications that arise out of eating, for which chocolate, for example, combines both pleasure and guilt.[35] There are, however, other stresses that straddle these divisions. Growing up for young girls, for example, entails entering the world of food as women with women's domestic roles. In this context, the familiar and familial demands arising out of the gender division of labour around food themselves provide a motive for not growing up. Who wants to take responsibility for providing food, with all the attendant judgements and responses delivered by the rest of the family, especially the husband, over the suitability and success of meals, quite apart from the resentments that this engenders in the provider around what is treated as a mundane task. It involves a complex of emotions and practices that can be observed and participated in by children with the potential for considerable foreboding about future roles.[36] Amongst other hypotheses, Devine and Olson (1992) suggest that women perceive different food roles at different life stages, provide care for the nutritional needs of others at their own expense, use food to keep the family peace, especially at meal-times, and are often strained by the conflict between health goals and their husbands' food preferences.

Yet a further index of the stresses attached to eating is the generality of the symptoms across the population as a whole, even if with different degrees of incidence, as is apparent for obesity. This is so even for anorexia. Whilst heavily associated with young, white, middle- and upper-class females, it is not confined to them.[37] It is generally reckoned that 10 per cent of anorexics are men (Butler, 1988). Further, Davis and Yager (1992, p. 389) give an account of the literature, mostly based on a survey of case studies, showing that

> Ethnically diverse patients describe symptoms and associated findings similar to those in typical Westernized Caucasian patients. Similarly, the number of cases reported in studies of bulimia among non-clinical populations of Asians, Africans, African-Americans, Hispanics, Indians, and Arabs were often reported to be within the ranges reported for non-clinical studies of controlled Caucasian female samples in Westernized countries.

Not surprisingly, eating disorders are found in third world countries where western culture, or the pressures to adopt it, is present (Wilfley and Rodin, 1995; Khandelwal et al., 1995). For minority ethnic communities, conflict between cultures is conducive to stress around eating (Furnham and Patel, 1994; Crago et al., 1996).

Other studies have noted the increasing incidence of anorexia amongst boys, and cases to be found amongst the old (Cosford and Arnold, 1992; Hall and Driscoll, 1993), possibly overlooked previously since presumed to be due to other causes. There have even been cases amongst the blind (Sharp, 1993), indicative of a more limited role for body image. Previously, it had been assumed that black women were less susceptible to anorexia than white women in view of the different ideologies surrounding beauty and gender roles, but some studies now find young black girls exhibiting a greater drive to thinness than their white counterparts.[38] Recent studies have also focused upon the impact of gender and of sexual orientation upon eating disorders. Not surprisingly, sexual orientation tends to moderate the effect of gender on the incidence of eating disorders (gay men more susceptible to anorexia, gay women less so, for example), and this is usually associated with the impact on body image (Schneider et al., 1995; French et al., 1996).[39] What is equally significant is the presence of the conditions across all types of sexual orientation.

From the review of the literature so far, a number of general observations emerge. First, it is highly concerned with correlations between a variety of symptoms of eating disorders and other factors, whether physical, psychological or sociocultural. There are so many variables from which to choose and such an apparent heterogeneity of linkages, especially – as is common – where small samples are taken, that such research can prosper without limit.[40] In a more sophisticated form, simple correlations have given way to multiple regressions. These, in turn, are found to be inadequate and are enriched by longitudinal studies which are also endowed with the benefits of untying causation from correlation once the former is associated with the chronological sequence of events. A occurred before, and is correlated with, B, and hence A caused B. In the case of obesity, for example, Friedman and Brownell (1995) identify three generations of studies – simple and multiple regressions for correlates and generational studies for causation – to sort out who suffers and why. For Wren and Lask (1993, pp. 69–70):

> The search for a single cause for eating disorders has largely been abandoned. . . . The effort to understand the aetiology of eating disorders lies therefore not in pinning down a simple pathogenesis nor simply identifying risk factors but in understanding how the various *predisposing*, *precipitating* and *perpetuating* factors interact and develop over time to produce the condition.

Such an approach not only looks for correlations between variables over time but also suggests the potential for different dispositions and pathways to eating disorders.[41] Thus, low esteem as a schoolchild leads to later eating problems (Button *et al.*, 1996).[42]

Whilst the literature has become more extensive in the range of variables considered and the inclusion of the passage of time, it does not otherwise address issues of causation. Through reviewing the literature, the purpose of this section has been to establish that food is stressful in a wide variety of ways. It is as important not to stereotype the symptoms associated with eating disorders as it is not to stereotype the victims. There is a continuum of individual behaviour in response to these stresses. When someone who becomes anorexic, for example, is socially defined around blurred boundaries. Nonetheless, these do exist and can be identified most obviously with body-weight. There also appears, after a certain point, to be an intensification of the physical and emotional symptoms, leading to models of anorexia which depend upon the notions of stages of development. Nonetheless, it is important to recognise that appetite is not lost in advanced stages of anorexia, except as a physiological consequence. Rather, contrary to Freud, who wished to interpret anorexia as a loss of appetite derived from a displaced form of denying sexuality, there is a strengthening of the resolve not to succumb to the dictates of appetite. Anorexia involves the denial, not the loss, of appetite, all the more remarkable given the wasting of the body. Similarly, those who are obese have not lost, nor are they unaware of, the pressures upon them to diet. Indeed, they may well experience them even more powerfully than those who are not overweight.

This points to a peculiarity of much of the literature on anorexia – its neglect of the *compulsion to eat*. Whilst it is fully recognised that the condition is a consequence of the tensions between the imperatives to eat and not to eat, the one is taken for granted and set aside just as the other is subject to detailed analysis. To repeat, there is a tension, however tight, for us all between the imperatives to eat and to deny ourselves food.[43] For anorexia, the tension is dramatic, even if it is resolved in a particular extreme form, denial of appetite. Possibly for this reason, because appetite is taken as natural or normal, and because of the priority to determine treatment to reverse denial, analytical attention has been heavily skewed away from the causes of the compulsion to eat that the anorexic is seeking to overcome. By the same token, the analysis of obesity – a resolution of the tensions both to eat and to diet at the other extreme to anorexia – tends to neglect the compulsion to diet. The two conditions are not, however, perfect mirror images of one another because the compulsion to eat is taken as natural, and obesity is perceived as involving lack of control. On the other hand, anorexia is understood as the denial of the natural inclination to eat and the exaggerated exercise of control. Nonetheless, the overweight tend to deny that they eat too much, often dramatically under-reporting what they do consume. Anorexics exaggerate what they have consumed, especially the calories contained in those foods associated with being fattening.[44]

It is not being argued that the pressures to eat are not recognised in studies of anorexia, only that they are endowed with a secondary status in view of the transparent outcome that they have been overwhelmed. Their significance is even pushed to the fore, even in narrowly defined medical discourse. It is known that force-feeding or browbeating can be counterproductive, precisely because it intensifies the pressures that produce the denial of appetite. Further, bulimia has been coupled with anorexia, even though it is associated with food binges and may not lead to abnormal body-weight.[45]

Anorexia, bulimia and obesity, then, although they are accompanied by, and displaced upon, other stresses, are all alternative, if dramatic, resolutions of the tensions between whether to eat or not.[46] Significantly, because anorexia and obesity present very different symptoms and induce very different treatments, there is a rationale for understanding them as deriving from separate causes. Further, the earlier coupling together of anorexia and bulimia has presented problems of diagnosis,[47] especially of the latter, since it can be associated with normal weight even though it shares with anorexia the aversion to eating or its consequences. Consequently, there is a desire to diagnose and treat anorexia and bulimia separately, reinforcing the notion of different origins for different eating disorders. Recognising that this is in part fallacious, as well as the wide and widening range of socioeconomic characteristics and individual stresses with which these eating disorders are associated, opens up the problem of explaining the social origins of these stresses and why they should have intensified.

From sociocultural to socioeconomic approaches

In the literature that lies outside the mainstream of psychology and psychiatry, the first step is taken in interpreting eating disorders as a disturbance to the individual psyche in which eating behaviour is the displaced form of some other neurosis. As previously seen, this displacement can incorporate factors such as the role of family interaction (and the wish of the anorexic to exercise control, power or independence), or broader social imperatives concerning the compulsion to attain an externally determined notion of the ideal physical form of the, generally female, body.[48] Even if anorexia, for example, is merely interpreted as an extreme form of dieting in pursuit of an ideal, thin body, the determinants and meaning of the latter are readily, perhaps even more so than for anorexia itself, recognisable to the social theorist to be socially and historically determined, not least in the shifting image of the ideal body shape.[49] Effectively, the explanation for anorexia itself, like the syndrome it seeks to explain, becomes displaced from the individual to society and to the latter's shifting norms. As Bordo (1993, p. 45) suggests by way of parody: 'What passed for cultural analysis were statistical studies demonstrating the dwindling proportions of *Playboy* centrefolds and Miss America winners throughout the 1980s.'[50]

Even where social determinants of anorexia have been placed in the foreground and pursued to greater depths, as in feminist analyses, they have tended to be counterposed unproblematically from an analytical point of view to individual needs, motivations and behaviour. It is a simplification, but not a dramatic one, to characterise much feminist understanding of anorexia as a particular form of (particular) young women's confrontation with patriarchy. But, as MacSween (1993) has thoroughly demonstrated, this has entailed an inadequate examination of the social determinants of anorexia because of the unexplored privileging of certain categories, especially the definition of the individual as self and as a body.[51] Why are modern women concerned with self as an individual in conflict with an external society, and why does that concern focus upon bodily form?

That these are peculiarly contemporary concerns is particularly well illustrated by the tendency to conflate any form of extreme food denial as belonging to the same species of anorexia, so that the condition can, erroneously, be traced back historically.[52] Increasingly, especially with the introduction of cultural and social factors in comprehending eating disorders, today's anorexia and increasingly the other eating disorders are seen as distinct from similar conditions in patients or individuals in the past. Thus, as MacSween (1993, p. 23) shows, the holy anorexics of feudal times employed a different concept of their bodies and their relation to the external world. For, in the fourteenth century, 'it was the *world*, not just food, which [Saint] Catherine [of Siena] rejected'. And it is a different world with a different place for the individual and for gender within it.[53] Indeed, the religious content of anorexia is notable for its absence in contemporary society, almost inevitably so given the preoccupation with the body as appearance rather than as unholy or devilish flesh.[54] Otherwise, the feudal and bourgeois forms of anorexia could only be conflated through a peculiar commitment to 'dieting for Jesus'.[55] More specifically, as Lester (1995) sharply demonstrates, the modern preoccupation with body image, with accompanying concerns with diet, calories and weight, is notably absent in the past, where goals were religiously moti- vated. On the other hand, Bemporad (1996) posits a transhistorical understanding of anorexia through perceiving it as the socially specific outcome of the conflict faced by women between the Cthonian (pro-creative, biological) and the Apollonian (cultural) ideals that prevail.

Remarkably, especially in view of the historically shifting mean- ings of the body, the insights of social theorists such as Foucault and Habermas have been relatively rare in their application to eating disorders.[56] This is despite a healthy literature in which these two writers are confronted with (their neglect of) feminism,[57] and despite Foucault's central preoccupation with the body, sexuality, medicine and insanity. Specifically, much light can be shed on eating disorders through Foucault's notion that the body is a primary site for the exercise of power with corresponding knowledges and practices, especially in conjunction with Habermas's emphasis upon legitimation and the potential for collective and individual cultures of resistance.

More generally, in view of the range of factors that have been identified as significant in eating disorders, the scope for the application of social theory is more or less unlimited. Thus, Sobal (1995), for example, examines obesity in terms of its medicalisation. The same theme is taken up by Malson (1998) in recognising that anorexia is open to a multiplicity of sociocultural concerns in constituting what it is to be a woman in late twentieth-century western culture. Eating disorders are a response to the exercise of power and control as well as socially constructed meanings of these in the minds and bodies of individual subjectivity. For others, eating disorders represent ritual (and a symbolic encounter and return from death) (Garrett, 1996, 1997), fetishism linking food and sex (Gamman and Makinen, 1994), and the construction of identity through thinness (Hesse-Biber, 1996). Further, as Bray (1996) observes, the anorexic body can be constructed and deconstructed, by self and others. She provides twenty such readings that have been made, warning against exclusive preoccupation with women's responses to media portrayals of female images and suggesting the incorporation of the medical and other discourses attached to calories, fitness and weightwatching. By the same token, the different and complex readings of the body give rise to different diagnoses and treatments as well, (Jarman et al., 1997), with extensive varieties of dietary regimes to attract and motivate those who attempt to read and reshape the body that is their text (Hopwood, 1995).

However, one of the difficulties created for the study of eating disorders of this type, as well as for others that move beyond an exclusive focus upon the individual, is how to reconcile social factors with individual incidence. This is implicitly recognised by Campbell's (1995) survey of our knowledge in the context of asking what would constitute an explanation for eating disorders. His conclusion is most revealing: 'The short answer must be that we do not yet know, and there does not appear to be much agreement

about what we are looking for' (p. 61). He finds research to be fragmented, without systematic models, and drawn from psychiatry and
psychology, supplemented by the notion of an abused role of women
within a male-dominated western society.

Not surprisingly, as this illustrates, the sorts of answers that we
obtain about the causes of eating disorders depend heavily upon the
sorts of questions that we ask, the meaning that these endow to
eating disorders, and the depth, direction and scope with which we
pursue answers. Consequently, our explanations are very different
according to whether we focus upon sexuality, body image,
maturing, self-esteem and control, patriarchy, physiology, and so on
– and how we site these factors within and across disciplinary
boundaries. In addition, the potential for stress displacement creates
the potential for any number and selection of such factors to be
causally connected with one another. The difficulty lies less, then, in
identifying factors to blame for eating disorders and more in
selecting between them and how they fit together causally.

The focus here will be concerned with three distinct but closely
related and central questions – Why women? Why thinness increasingly as the prevailing norm of female body image? And why food?
Even though these do not fill out the domain of eating disorders –
there are other sufferers and forms of suffering – light will be shed
on eating disorders more generally. And only by addressing these
three questions together will a more complete understanding of
eating disorders potentially emerge. It will prove possible by
relating the three questions to what has already been shown to be
crucial to eating disorders – the simultaneous and competing pressures both to eat and to diet. In approaching these pressures
through political economy, it is necessary to identify and explain
the strength of the commercial pressures involved and why they
should prove so effective and, hence, disastrous.

Beginning with the question 'Why women?', as has been
observed, the strains placed upon women in contemporary capitalism have intensified despite an expansion in the boundaries of
economic and social welfare that appear to be, and are, open to
them. The increasing generality of this female experience is testified
to not only in the extent of emancipation, however much unequal in
practice, but also in the remarkable changes in female labour
market participation over the post-war period, especially for
married women. To summarise desperately my argument elsewhere
(Fine, 1992), there is a strong logical connection, with a distinct
chronology, between the rise and predominance of mass 'Fordist'

production, falls in fertility and family size, growing female labour market participation, the drive to mass consumption, and the growing role of the welfare state in education and health. In this light, in the compulsion both to work and to consume, capitalist modernity creates stresses for us all, but particularly for women in view of inherited roles around motherhood and sexuality, which they must combine within the context of additional responsibilities and norms. Much of the literature discussed previously has observed the tensions that have arisen and connected them to eating disorders.

Although it will not be attempted in detail here, an explanation for the history and contemporary incidence of eating disorders is suggested by these insights. Crudely, it might help to explain why anorexia, for example, should first emerge as a modern condition around the turn of the century amongst relatively affluent young women in an unwitting anticipation of the more widespread and rather different stresses underlying future eating disorders. Further, the paradox is resolved – that anorexia, or non-consumption, should afflict the wealthier, whilst obesity, or overconsumption, should be more prevalent amongst the poorer within wealthier societies. Those who are better-off reject (the commercial pressures to) gratification altogether, with dramatic results in the case of food, whilst such rejection of gratification is not open to the poorer sections of the population, for whom gratification through food is a feasible compensation for their relative poverty.[58]

Clearly, this discussion of the shifting position of women can shed light on the other two issues – thinness and food. Commercialisation has been extended to sexuality and carries with it the compulsion to mould body image. Food occupies a key position in women's responsibilities. Further, with the expanding role for women in the workforce, there is, however unequally, a mixing of traditional male and female roles and, hence, representations – as has been observed in the occasional androgyny of fashion and commercials, partly as a consequence of thinness, boyishness, girlishness, at one extreme, and partly as women take on male attributes (shoulder pads, for example, and power dressing more generally) at the other.

Approaching eating disorders, then, from the perspective of a more general political economy of women does provide considerable insights. But it cannot satisfactorily address our two other issues of thinness and food. For the former, there is no reason why commercial pressures and shifting roles should privilege thin over fat.

Indeed, the latter might be presumed to be more appropriate to a commercial world engaged in promoting the imperatives of consumption. And why should food be privileged as the pivot upon which so much stress is balanced rather than other commodities for which there are equally powerful pressures to produce, sell and consume? It is the latter question that is addressed first.

Why food?

Despite – in the context of anorexia, for example – the importance of the pressures to eat and to diet, the commercial pressures involved have only been identified in the most superficial way in the literature, especially when set against the displaced emotional content of food, which is seen as serving gratification in a wide variety of ways – control, self-identity, comfort, reward, ritual, and so on. In short, the political economy of food is notable for its absence. It is generally raised only in a token fashion. Romeo (1986, p. 18) provides a typical example: 'There has been a proliferation and acceptance of junk foods and fast food chains. Food is ever-present in our affluent society. Women are torn between two opposing forces: the stimulation to eat and constant pressure to be thin.' This is followed by silence on the role of the affluent society as a force presumed, in this instance, to lie behind the stimulation to eat. For MacSween (1993, p. 174), it is observed that 'the frantic pursuit of beauty and the frantic pursuit of profit walk hand in hand',[59] but this is taken no further and not linked to the frantic pursuit of profit through selling food (with its negative connotations for beauty, unless they be contradictory, as for diet foods).[60] Gordon (1990) refers to the greater variety of foods and its market fragmentation between the discount and the fashionable segments. He observes that 'eating, even excessive eating, is therefore good for business', and recognises that this conflicts with the imperatives of the fashion and dieting sectors: 'But while overconsumption is encouraged by an economy whose hunger for profits seems limitless, the ultimate contradiction that leads us back to eating disorders is the simultaneous demand, also economically promoted (but by a different industry) to be thin' (pp. 115–16).

Similarly, whilst Orbach (1993) places enormous emphasis on the role of consumer society, this is not matched in analytical content since the notion is mentioned on only seven pages of her book. Indeed, her concern is more with the symbolic content embodied in food, appealing to the nostrum that you are what you eat, pointing to food as a status symbol comparable to a car, and the tension between aesthetic and utilitarian attitudes to food (p. 32). But how do these undeniable aspects of food relate to the tensions between eating and not eating? Nothing more is done than to imply a tightening of those tensions through the increasing symbolic significance of food. Yet this needs to be socially and historically delimited and tied specifically to food rather than to other commodities. Whilst the literature is extensive in pointing the finger of blame at the food and dieting industries, and forging connections between them and eating disorders, little attention is paid, other than at the empirical level, to explaining why these industries have emerged to prominence in the way that they have.

This is especially so given the social and historical incidence of anorexia. As Brumberg (1988) observes, the condition was seen as emerging in Italy only as a consequence of post-war affluence. As food became a common resource in the middle-class household, it was more amenable for use in emotional manipulation. For 'During the Great Depression and World War I, in times of scarcity, voluntary food refusal had little efficacy as an emotional strategy and anorexic girls were a relative rarity in American clinical practices' (p. 10).

In short, general economic conditions have to allow for food to be sufficiently plentiful, taking account of inequalities in income, for it to serve as much more than a necessity. Thus, following Elias, and in a complex argument drastically simplified here, Mennell (1987) views the civilising of appetite as the promotion of self-control and its association with delicacy, once food is sufficiently plentiful. In the twentieth century, this becomes translated into dieting and the drive for thinness as a form of sexual attraction. But it is also necessary to explain why twentieth-century affluence is also associated with the compulsion to eat. Here, the idea of consumer society does its work – profitability is dependent upon sales, which are sought through manipulative advertising. The same productive powers that give rise to a surfeit of food, at least to a minority of the world's population, generate the commercial pressures for excessive consumption.

Consequently, as an object of consumption, food is open to commercial pressures like all other commodities. It does, however, have certain characteristics that distinguish it.[61] Whilst, in a previous era of limited food suppliers, meal patterns were laid down and evolved, the era of mass consumption has subjected these patterns to considerable erosion through creation of the continuous availability of eating and drinking, and the corresponding availability of food and food outlets, even to those with moderate income. Within the home, dried, frozen, canned and other forms of foods, together with fridges, freezers, microwaves and other domestic durables, imply the omnipresence of food. Much the same is true out of the home, with the vast range of snacks, retailers, and the variety of establishments for eating out, including fast food as well as conventional restaurants spread over an ever-widening variety of cuisines.[62] Both in the manufacturing and retailing of food, the extent of choice and flexibility in products verges on the unlimited, with the potential to accommodate almost any taste or affect, displaced or not, through variability in the product and in its representation through advertising.

Given these developments, it is hardly surprising that the compulsion to eat, and its promotion by the imperative of profitability attached to the food industries, should be readily acknowledged. What is less satisfactory is the neglect of the ways in which the food industry has evolved in conjunction with other closely related factors to create such an intense pressure – through hypermarket retailing, the range of products and opportunities to eat, the drive for convenience, the shifting forms of cooking and eating habits, and the capacity to incorporate meanings into food products through advertising – to be healthy, sophisticated, traditional or whatever.[63]

But matters are not so simple. However well it is defined and understood,[64] consumer society applies in principle to all commodities. This means that the pressures to purchase and to consume are not specific and confined to food alone. Indeed, such pressures for food are liable to be constrained by the competing demands from all other commodities, as in obsessional shopping leading to credit card abuse and even shoplifting where this is not even a consequence of poverty-driven need.

It might be argued that food is different because of the limited capacity to consume given physiological constraints. Without coming to any harm, you can have as many or as few trinkets or cars as you like – even as many pairs of shoes, despite, like Imelda Marcos, only having one pair of feet. The same does not appear to apply to food, which, presumably, explains why obsessional behaviour around it is treated as a medical condition. It has been popular to argue that the limits to the capacity to consume food, and a corresponding falling off of the proportion of expenditure with economic affluence, is itself a reason for over-processing in order that more value and profit can be added to the manufacturer's purse. Whilst this argument is not convincing in such a direct form, it does point to the potential of capitalists to enhance profitability by transforming the nature or the image of their products. Foods can be advertised, be made more sophisticated or be attached to other activities, such as preparation avoidance as in convenience foods or eating out. Thus, it follows that the commercially generated pressures to eat are not always direct – as more or less extreme forms of the imperative to 'stop me and buy one'.[65] More generally, the pressures to eat filter in complex ways through the food, cultural and socioeconomic systems as a whole, and in ways which will be differentiated both by type of food and by the individual socioeconomic status of the consumer.

All of this, however, only provides an explanation for obesity arising out of the commercial pressures to eat even if it potentially has its counterpart in the guilt attached to obsessive eating given the presence of health or other concerns about weight. There are also implications for which foods are liable to figure in eating disorders, but not why the compulsion to consume should be more extreme than for commodities other than food. The connections to other eating disorders, and their dependence upon the compulsion to diet, have not been established through political economy. By focusing on the food system alone, we can only establish the commercial pressures behind the compulsion to eat, privileging obesity amongst eating disorders and only partially explaining the symptoms of the latter.

An obvious response to this conundrum is to point to the pressures generated by the dieting industry and its counterpart in fashion. There is no problem in identifying the commercial interests promoting the pressures not to eat. Dieting is itself a profit-making enterprise, worth $5 billion in the United States according to Brumberg (1988). Further, as is explicitly and frequently recognised by feminism, the fashion industry in the twentieth century has encouraged the goal of thinness, even though the ideal body is itself variable over time (often seen itself as a way in which fashion can market itself by rendering existing clothes obsolescent).

The problem, then, is less one of explaining why there are commercial pressures both to eat and to diet than how it is possible for them to co-exist and prosper despite their apparent incompatibility. For the intensification of the strains over whether to eat or not is highly dependent upon the commercial viability of both food and diet industries and, especially for the latter, related commercial ventures. Whilst, once pointed out, it is blindingly obvious that eating disorders depend upon the tensions between the pressures to eat and to diet, their compatibility at the economic level is far from apparent. It is as if dieting and related fashion industries are as 'natural' as food industries, like bread and butter, or, more exactly, bread and not butter.

To make the point clear, consider other examples from the world of commodities. The commercial pressures to smoke are heavily promoted by advertising, and this is a contested terrain since the tobacco industry is acutely aware that its profitability is threatened by restrictions on the ways in which it can promote itself. Whilst it might be argued that there is an anti-smoking 'industry', significantly, it is not a commercial venture, with few exceptions. And if it were, it could almost certainly only prosper at the expense of smoking, which would, then, render it redundant if successful.[66]

There is a simple observation being made here – the commercial drive to consumption cannot be based primarily on an anti-consumption ethic, although, by way of exception, anti-commercialism and anti-consumerism can be employed, para-doxically, as a selling point, as in the image of the home-made or in products designed to curb or modify consumption habits. These products are, however, necessarily derivative and can only persist by dwelling parasitically upon the continuing success of the commercial products that they putatively seek to displace. Such products would inevitably prove to be victims of their own success, like a totally effective vaccine. It necessarily follows that the scope for stress to arise out of anti-consumptionism is generally limited, especially socially and with the passage of time.

Consider, however, a slightly different type of example. There is a tension, often felt by individual consumers at practical and ideological levels, between utilising public and private transport and the modes that they assume – walking, cycling, car, bus, and so on. The distribution of these different forms of transport across the slightly different and fuzzy divide between commercial and non-commercial provision has not created an epidemic of individual 'transport disorders' despite, at the time of writing, the creation of a 'media scare' around road rage. In this case, there are tensions around public and private forms of transport, and commercial and non-commercial provision; at times, these tensions are resolved by expansion of one at the expense of others, at other times through expansion of more than one with the potential for excessive consumption of transport with deleterious social impacts – in overcrowding and on the environment, for example.

The compulsions to eat and not to eat combine features from both of these examples. Commercially, it has proved possible to accommodate both even though they appear to be incompatible. This is because not eating has taken the commercial form of dieting so that a high proportion of women are both overweight (overeating) and dieting (as if not eating). The potential for this apparent inconsistency to materialise warrants a discussion of body image, and thinness, in more detail.

Why thinness? Contradictions in the political economy of body image

As already observed, much emphasis in examining eating disorders is placed on the impact of the goals that women have for their bodies and their own images of them. Apart from advertising to promote both eating and dieting, the media representation of the slender female body is pervasive.[67] As Hesse-Biber (1996) puts it, there is a cult of thinness which has been commercialised. It is attached to a general dissatisfaction with being overweight, leading to a preoccupation with dieting, and there is also a tendency for women to overestimate weight both absolutely and relative to social averages (as opposed to media images of the ideal woman). Because successful dieting represents control, lack of success signifies loss of self-esteem.[68]

Such observations have led to the view that women have a chronic problem with weight that leads to an outbreak of dieting from time to time. It is as if media and sexist pressures lead to continuous dissatisfaction with the (idea of the) body, in extreme forms in the case of anorexia where even the starving body can be perceived as overweight. This is not, however, an accurate understanding of women's images of their bodies. As Myers and Biocca (1992) show, body image is extremely elastic. In particular, the degree of image distortion can be reduced, or even reversed, according to what has been represented on television. Not surprisingly, viewing fashion models or the portrayal of the ideal, thin woman in programmes designed to titillate men is liable to induce feelings of being overweight. But the effect of other programmes in which other roles are played out can have the opposite effect, leading viewers to be less conscious of weight and able to perceive themselves as having a more appropriate body image. Such shifts in self-perception can follow from watching a mere thirty-minute television programme. The heavy presence of (shifting) body images which encourage notions of being overweight and the imperative to be slim, together with other social pressures to conform to be attractive to men, should not lead us to overlook the co-existence of other images alongside or, more aptly, in conflict with these.

Indeed, the formation of body image is itself extremely complex, as is its relationship to eating behaviour. First, it involves different media (Harrison and Cantor, 1997) distinguishing body dissatisfaction and the drive for thinness, for example, with magazines much more prominent than television in promoting the latter. Second, the false perception of body image involves processing images, comparing them with perception of self, others and ideals, each of which has to be formed. Distortions can occur at any of these stages and can vary in incidence and over time, across those suffering different types of eating disorders or not (Szymanski and Cash, 1995; Beebe et al., 1996; Szymanski and Seime, 1997; Cash and Deagle, 1997).[69]

In any case, there are, then, plenty of body images in the media which do *not* appear to create tensions around being overweight. Otherwise, this might discourage regular viewing; the viewer can hardly be made to feel uncomfortable all of the time. Indeed, it would be a peculiar food advertisement that employed images of unduly thin (or fat) people in the attempt to peddle its wares – other than for diet foods (as in before and after body images!). For either thin (potential target body image) or fat (failure to hit target) could be counterproductive to sales. Those tensions are to be found in various proportions, and in extremely complex ways, in each and every food and in the images attached to them.

Nor does this tension derive simply from image or culture. As argued in Chapter 4, how we understand food is a consequence of the *interaction* of the information system around food (media, 'common sense', health campaigns, and so on) and the food system itself, which, understood as the production, distribution, retailing, preparation and consumption of food, generates its own forms of knowledge. The corollary drawn here is that the individual is not simply faced with a tension between eating and not eating food, but that foods (and practices around them) already differentially embody that tension (and other symbolisms).[70] In short, and it is a fantastic deception in the modern age of reason, the dieting industry allows us to believe that there are foods that we can consume without really having eaten. In this extreme form, it is easy to understand why there are commercial pressures both to eat and not to eat, since a form of compatibility has been forged between the two – dieting as eating, but not really. More generally, against the weight of the commercial pressure to eat, a whole range of industries have emerged that deny that they involve eating or that they can compensate for it. It is precisely these industries, as discussed earlier, that give rise to the notion that the body is malleable and a personal responsibility.

This discussion can be illustrated in a number of ways, not least in the meanings attached to food by anorexics. Bowyer (1988, p. 161) suggests that 'there is no typical profile for the dietary pattern of the eating-disordered patient'. However, this refers more to the nutritional content of foods than to foods themselves. It is found that foods that are conceived as 'good' are often consumed in disproportionate quantities. How much has been eaten is also open to miscalculation (Jansen, 1996). The eating patterns of anorexics follow the fashions prescribed by nutritional recommendations and the foods associated with slimming. Vegetarianism is often embraced, but chocolate and cakes prove particularly troublesome. Thus, the fact that foods already carry a variety of contradictory messages concerning their impact on health, weight, and so on, and are produced and sold as such, must itself be a source of tension over the impetus to eat or not. It is perhaps not surprising that excessively strong coffee is frequently taken in large quantities, unsweetened and without milk; in this way, it is an apparently uncomplicated beverage, whose content is known, with the added effect, especially when drunk very hot, of counteracting hunger sensations.[71]

The tension between eating and not eating can be embodied in particular products, and can even be used as a selling point. Because you should not really be consuming this, you will indulge yourself by doing so. This has been neatly captured in the UK advertisement for cream cakes, coining the slogan, 'Naughty but Nice'. But exactly the same phenomenon can be found in the construction of diet across a number of products. As Heasman (1990) has shown, the market for 'lite' products has grown out of a nutritional concern for products with fewer calories, or specific nutrients such as fats or sugars. They are motivated by the idea of displacing 'heavy' products. In practice, however, the result has been to allow oneself either a *carte blanche* to eat as much of the lite products as one likes, or to justify the consumption of other, heavy products in addition. A particular example is provided by dairy products. In the UK,

THE POLITICAL ECONOMY OF EATING DISORDERS

skimmed milks now occupy more than 50 per cent of the market. However, there has been a simultaneous growth in high fat content dairy products, such as desserts and fancy cheeses. Our research (as reported in Fine *et al.*, 1996, Chapter 12) shows that those who are most prominent in taking up healthy, creamless milk are also first in the queue for the new and fancy dairy products!

We are now in a position to explain why thinness should have become, and been sustained as, the norm for women's body image. First of all, body image is attached to eating but it is more fundamentally derived from the fashion industry. As is readily recognised, this requires frequent change in order to promote renewed sales, and this can be achieved by cut, design, pattern, colour as well as by shape. Consequently, the imperatives of the fashion industry can only explain the change in body shape from time to time, not its being subordinated to thinness. Indeed, during the course of the first half of this century, it is fluctuations in ideal body shape that stand out in contrast to the earlier hegemony of more ample female forms, as indicative of opulence and femininity and in which body image was shaped as much through clothes as through the body itself.

The past fifty years, however, has witnessed the growth of industries attached to not eating, or the image of not eating, and these have forged a path which is almost entirely compatible with the eating industries – whether this be in diet foods or the fashions associated with clothes, health, exercise and medicine. For fashion, for example, to target a fuller figure on a consistent and persistent basis, it would need to overwhelm the cultural norms now established in those non-eating industries. But for the occasional exception,[72] it is as inconceivable as the food industry itself launching an explicit attack in part upon itself by preferring a fat to a thin figure. For the industry is already heavily implicated in the provision of 'non-foods', and it can readily draw upon its capacity to sell food by presenting body images that slightly lag to the more ample side of the norm set by fashion. In short, contemporary capitalism has discovered the best of all worlds. Its eating industries are prospering as never before. But so are its non-eating industries, and the two feed upon one another, closely integrated and mutually supportive. The outcome is an ideal of thinness that has only served to reinforce and intensify the tensions between eating and non-eating that have been so conducive to the eating disorders of affluence.

Concluding observations

Our work has been based on the idea that food consumption should be understood in terms of differentiated food systems. This insight has now been brought to bear upon the analysis of eating disorders. Once it is recognised that they are the complex outcome of the pressures both to eat and to diet, then these two pressures can be usefully interrogated from the perspective of political economy. The restructuring of food systems within and between each of their constituent components will reflect and have an impact upon the tensions between eating and dieting irrespective of, but in conjunction with, their sociocultural incidence through the psychologies of particular individuals. In this respect, as in others, different foods carry different potential meanings, and these can only be uncovered by reference to the food systems to which they belong.

But the understanding of eating disorders as arising out of contradictory tensions can, indeed must, itself be used as a model for understanding the functioning of food systems. As argued at the outset of this chapter, eating disorders are not appropriately set aside and isolated as analytically deviant from normal eating. Eating disorders are to a large extent the outcome of socioeconomic pressures that are experienced by us all in common. Consequently, food systems should be understood as arising out of contradictory tensions. For they are themselves subject to conflicting forces which give rise to complex structures and outcomes – the technological 'treadmill', vertical and horizontal integration, standardisation and flexibility in products and processing, own-label versus branded, and so on, quite apart from the pressures to eat and to abstain that arise directly at the level of consumption. Whether in formulating medical diagnosis and treatment for eating disorders or food policy for those other less deviant forms of the diseases of affluence, it will be essential to identify the full range of factors involved and how they interact even if they are not directly attached to the critical individual symptoms observed. In other words, once it is recognised that eating disorders are associated with the socially created pressures both to eat and to diet, then there are two questions to be addressed by political economy. First, how are those pressures linked to other economic forces and developments? Second, how do these factors interact with one another and influence and interact with other determinants of diet?

4

DIGESTING THE FOOD AND INFORMATION SYSTEMS

Introduction

Well over a decade ago, Budd and McCron (1982) were reporting on research into the relationship between mass communication and health education. The context of their contribution was one in which the provision of health care was switching from a model of the delivery of curative medicine to one of preventative medicine:

> The framework for discussing health issues has given prominence to scientific research, technological development, medical expertise and a hospital-based, curative model of health care . . . it is now increasingly recognised that the major advances in public health, previously attributed to scientific advance, are more likely to stem from socio-environmental developments, such as improved sanitation, nutrition, housing and working conditions, and greater inputs from professionals in the fields of medicine and health education.
>
> (p. 190)

Consequently, somewhat paradoxically, as health care was being politicised as being dependent on social rather than medical intervention, it was increasingly subject to an ideology in which it was seen as the responsibility of the individual – the need, for example, for the individual to avoid smoking and excessive alcohol consumption, to take exercise and avoid obesity. Such individual responsibility depended upon the public being properly informed about what was healthy and what was unhealthy so that they could adopt appropriate behaviour.

Budd and McCron highlight the simplistic models previously

used to promote health education, one in which 'correct' information was made available for the public to absorb and act upon as it pleased. Drawing upon mass communication research, they point to the inadequacy of this as a model of how individuals form health knowledge and behave accordingly. They also deplore the extent to which their earlier, similar conclusions had been subject to resistance from practitioners within the field of health education.

The purpose here is not to bring this story forward to the present day but rather to observe the parallels with education around healthy eating and food choice. Essentially, if not explicitly, Budd and McCron employ a model in which health education is a consequence of the interaction of two systems: the system of health care itself and the system of mass communication around health (necessarily broadly interpreted to include 'common knowledge', for example, and by no means confined to educational campaigns). In the case of food choice, there has also been a major change of thinking over recent years. Nutrition education is concerned with the dissemination of knowledge based on current human nutrition thinking (CHNT). It is influenced by government advisory bodies which publish reports including dietary guidelines and goals. In the UK, two influential advisory reports have been published which make recommendations about diet in the UK: the National Advisory Committee on Nutrition Education (NACNE) report was published as a discussion document in 1983 by the Health Education Authority; and the Committee on Medical Aspects of Food Policy report on Diet and Cardiovascular Disease (COMA) was published in 1984.

The NACNE (1983) report was significant because it was the first government statement to offer practical dietary goals and quantify the recommended amounts of dietary components. It also caused controversy because it was alleged that publication of the report was delayed.[1] Both the NACNE (1983) and COMA (1984) reports concentrate on the dietary components most likely to be implicated in causing disease. Both give recommendations for reduction in the consumption of fat, sugar and salt and increases for fibre. As deprivation and deficiencies in diet have become of less importance – the need to eat and drink enough of the right things – attention has turned to the diseases of affluence and longevity, associated with eating too much and of the wrong things. We all know now about cholesterol and fibre and their negative and positive implications for heart disease and cancer, respectively.

The drive towards healthier food has also become highly

politicised. It too is most appropriately understood in terms of a dual structure, the food system and its associated information system. Necessarily, however, each of these systems is different from the corresponding ones for health; transparently so in provision, for which one depends primarily on public, the other on private, supply. For this, as well as for other reasons, the origins of nutritional knowledge are also different. But, somewhat depressingly, if not surprisingly, a similar broad conclusion can be drawn for food as for health education – educating for healthy eating has been insufficiently sensitive to the diversity of the sources of food knowledge and their implications for food choice.[2]

There is a large and growing literature on the food information system.[3] It is extremely fragmented. At some times, it deals with scientific research; at others with the impact of leaflets on nutritional knowledge and food choice. By reviewing some of the literature, the complexity of the food information system will be revealed. An organising theme for this chapter is to examine the extent to which, and the way in which, adequate account has been taken of the interaction of the various parts of the food information system and of its own interaction with the food system itself. Too often, the focus of discussion has been too narrow, as if one particular aspect could be understood in isolation from others.

The pertinence of these opening remarks is well illustrated by Wiseman (1990), writing as a member of the UK Department of Health's Nutrition Unit. After providing an institutional description of the information system for nutrition and government's place within it, Wiseman asserts that 'The general philosophy of the current [Conservative] administration is very much that responsibility should lie with the individual.' But the individual must be properly informed:

> This means that the individual should be able to make an informed choice for his or her diet. In order for any choice to be informed, there must be enough information available, and the individual must be educated to interpret information usefully.

And there must be an appropriate choice of foods made available: 'It is the responsibility of MAFF [Ministry of Agriculture, Fisheries and Food] to ensure that a choice is available by ensuring a plentiful supply of wholesome food at affordable prices' (p. 399).

There is already considerable tension in the logic of Wiseman's position. The general philosophy (ideology) of the government in leaving matters to the individual is normally associated with the ideology of leaving them to the market. So no rationale is provided for MAFF to guarantee appropriate food supplies. Why should the market not do this by itself? The answer lies in the traditional role of MAFF in supporting the farming sector. In addition, the theory of 'unfolding', discussed in greater detail below, would suggest that nor need information be provided by the state, for this would emerge effortlessly through the beneficial advertising attached to the judicious exercise of consumer choice for healthy eating. Ultimately, then, by an implicit but arbitrary stance over when the market does work and when it does not, Wiseman perceives the substance of nutrition policy in the narrowest of terms: 'The output of nutrition policy is essentially the provision of information via labelling and education' (p. 400).

In effect, then, Wiseman takes those other actions of government which affect information about, and availability of, food as lying outside nutrition policy – this is even so for policies of the European Community, which is described as an 'outside influence'. This is presumably in order that such policies are not raised in the context of nutrition and health, especially the role of the food producers and their production of information. Consequently, not only is nutrition policy reduced to minuscule proportions, but extreme caution is exercised in deciding when to adopt it. Emphasis is placed on the uncertainty of scientific knowledge and its communication.

This would all be very well if the other sources of information and the other determinants of food choice proceeded along the same lines of scientific caution. But the struggle over informational determinants of food choice is not fought on such a level playing field. Whether employing health or other claims, producers do not display the compunctions associated with scientific verification when making or selling their products. And the same is true of other sources of nutritional information. It is precisely this issue that the then government, in supposedly relying on the individual, sought to avoid. Thus, Wiseman does call for the broadest under-standing of the determinants of food choice, but only to allow better coordination between those bodies that form the structure advising on nutrition policy:

'In order to make sensible decisions within this structure, we need information on what people eat, why they eat it, and how it affects them. The better that information system, the better the decisions that will be taken' (p. 400). Essentially, the information system around food has been reduced for practical purposes to the knowledge required by experts. In short, Wiseman seeks at most to provide the information about, and the choice of, foods so that individuals are able to be healthy consumers. As such the determinants of what people do eat and why is studiously ignored except in so far as it affects what information will be provided to the experts in pursuing their limited function in educating us towards a more beneficial dietary choice.

It might be thought that Wiseman's is an unrepresentative and extreme contribution, especially in the context of a government committed to the market and individual responsibility. To some extent this is true, but its approach does not depart enormously, from an analytical point of view, from much of the literature. Sources of information about food have traditionally been seen as either true (good) or bad (false) and as emanating either from non-commercial or commercial agencies, not necessarily respectively. By examining this framework for identifying the dissemination of food information, it will be shown that it is inadequate both in its understanding of the nature of food knowledge itself and in its understanding of the sources and effects of that knowledge. It is argued that the food information system must be understood in terms of its interaction with the food system, but where this has been done, even if implicitly, within the literature, it has been sorely inadequate.

The food information system and trickle-down of knowledge

The conventional view of the informational determinants of food choice is, as suggested in the introduction, based upon the way in which current human nutritional thinking (CHNT) is made available to, absorbed by, and acted upon by consumers. In effect, CHNT trickles down from scientists and ultimately ends up, symbolically speaking, in our stomachs. Suppose, for the moment, that this is an appropriate way to embark upon an understanding of the food information system. It still leaves room open for many a slip twixt science and lip, a journey that is worth traversing investigatively. Ashwell (1992) posits seven stages, for example, in the information transfer, starting within the first stage with scientific research papers and ending up within the last stage with gossip, custom and folklore.[4]

The first stage is with CHNT itself. What is it and where does it come from? CHNT evolves over time, partly in response to changing dietary problems, partly as a result of scientific advances, and certainly as a consequence of contestation between scientists engaged in research. Historically, there is a clear correspondence between the evolution of CHNT and specific stages in economic and, correspondingly, food development. James (1994), for example, identifies three revolutions in nutritional science: the first around micro-nutrients and the need for these to be consumed in sufficient quantities, as in the understanding of the origins of scurvy; the second around the adequate diet as provided for by the agricultural revolution following the Second World War; and the third corresponding to the diet-related diseases of affluence which have proved much more difficult to identify than the harmful effects of smoking, for example.[5] Inevitably, the particular directions taken by CHNT are heavily influenced by current, even if shifting, scientific norms,[6] by commercial interests within the food industry − it would take a drastic leap of faith to believe in the neutrality and altruism of scientists and for the content and results of their research to be unaffected by commercial needs − as well as by the concerns of government which are certainly no more guaranteed to be neutral and objective than for the private sector.[7]

Despite these features of CHNT, there is a remarkable unanimity in advice from the scientific establishment over the need for a number of changes in diet in order to avoid the western diseases of affluence (Cannon, 1992). This leads, then, to the second stage of how the information is supposedly disseminated. This varies according to the form taken by the media concerned. Direct provision of food information through health campaigns and/or health professionals is relatively rare, and the higher the professional in the hierarchy, the more the focus is liable to be upon diet in response to a medical condition rather than for general health. Nurses, for example, have better knowledge of dietary guidelines than doctors, consider them to be more important and are better able to communicate them (Rudat, 1992).

It is often recognised that the food information system is comprised of two components, the formal and the informal. The first of these is likely to be identified with nutrition education whose professed aim (according to BNF, DHSS, HEC, 1977, p. 3), is to 'provide people, particularly those who have the responsibility of feeding others or advising them about nutrition, with sufficient knowledge to equip them to take appropriate action for the maintenance of good health'. It involves the conscious attempt to effect the transmission of nutritional knowledge (either general or specialized) to consumers, caterers, food manufacturers, professional health-care workers and teachers. Organisations which have a formal responsibility for nutrition education in the UK include the Department of Education and Employment, the Department of Health, the Ministry of Agriculture, Fisheries and Food, the Health Education Authority, Area Health Authorities, and the British Nutrition Foundation (financed as a charity by the food industry). Other, often less formal, sources of nutrition education include professional journals (whether specialising in food or not), the media more generally, and commercial sponsorship or provision of nutrition information or healthy eating campaigns.

The most important source for communicating food information, however, is through the popular media such as TV, newspapers and magazines, for which, of course, advertising is often extremely important and inclusive of health claims. Leaving aside this commercial aspect for the moment, Ashwell (1992) argues that media presentation of CHNT is heavily distorted by *premature* reporting of scientific research in a *mischievous way*, not least as a means to *embellish* the newsworthiness of the stories involved.

Not surprisingly, then, the content of CHNT that is disseminated is distorted by the media. But equally important, the content cannot be communicated without being transformed, whether this be considered a distortion or not. For CHNT belongs to the realm of scientific discourse; it is not information as such which can be absorbed and acted upon by the general public. Consequently, CHNT is communicated in the form, for example, of dietary guidelines for overall consumption levels of fats, salt, and so on. Even these are not readily understood, and differences over what the guidelines should be and how they should be communicated, in health claims in advertising and on food labels, give rise to the notion that the experts disagree and cannot make up their minds. This might be true even if only reflecting a minority or fringe of disagreements, with marginal differences exaggerated for media hype or to protect commercial interests. Goldberg (1992) points to the varying difficulties of health messages, these often presuming a model of communicating advice rather than of generating understanding, and argues that some recommendations are easier to implement than others, and that messages are received through a wide range of media with different goals. An appeal is made for clear, consistent, focused, positive messages based on CHNT.

The third stage in the trickle-down is in how information is received. The vast majority of healthy eating advice concerns the composition of overall diet. Even where relatively simple messages are involved, such as eat less fat or eat more fresh fruit, these do not immediately translate into information about particular foods, which is the effective and disaggregated form in which diet is composed in practice. There are, then, two key issues involved here: the first is the divorce between nutrients and foods in the knowledge of consumers; the second is the divorce between knowledge of particular foods and overall diet: 'What is important to health is the whole composition of a person's diet, not the nutritional profile of individual foods that make up the diet' (Caswell and Padberg, 1992, p. 464). These issues have dominated, even if implicitly, much of the discussion over how to improve diet through nutritional information (Gillespie, 1987), for they concern how nutritional education should be communicated to be effective, what role commercial advertising can play in general and in health claims in particular, and what content and form should be taken by food labelling. Many food labels are difficult to understand, they have multiple purposes, and they are received and treated by consumers in different ways.[8]

Leaving this aside for the moment, the next stage in gaining food information concerns how the various messages are received. Partly reflecting the divorce between diet and nutrients but much more fundamentally in correspondence to the wide variety of social roles of food, healthy eating messages have to snuggle up to, or fight for a place with, an unlimited range of other individual understandings of food. This becomes acutely transparent in the case of eating disorders (see Chapter 3). In the realm of diet and health, the connection is jostled by confused perceptions over the distinction between health and beauty (for example, Henderson and Vickers, 1995; McKie et al., 1993). A healthy diet also competes for attention in the minds of, particularly female, providers with family roles in the provision of a proper meal and other eating functions (Devine and Olson, 1992). Vegetarians find different sets of food to be acceptable according to a varied range of ethics (animal rights), anxieties (food scares) and other health beliefs (Beardsworth and Keil, 1992; Richardson et al., 1994). Chapman and MacLean (1993) have discovered that junk food is associated with weight gain, friends, independence and guilt, whereas healthy foods are associated with weight loss, parental control and being at home. And so the different meanings of food could run on. A moment's reflection on how foods are advertised is sufficient to indicate that foods carry many meanings and that these are inextricably linked to one another, often in complex ways. Vegetarians, for example, are often seen and interpreted as both radical in being non-traditional but also as stolid or worthy in their altruism towards animals and hence to fellow human-beings (Dietz *et al.*, 1995). How nutritional information is received is not simple and unambiguous.

Closely related to, but separate from, the mixture of *meanings* of foods is the mixture of ways in which food information is incorporated. Kemm and Booth (1992, p. 119), for example, carefully distinguish between knowledge, beliefs and attitudes, each of which they seek to measure in order to be able to gauge the effectivity of healthy eating campaigns. Others have emphasised values and motivation. Although each of these terms has a different meaning from the others, as do information and education, this is itself indicative of the complexity of food knowledge. Particularly important is the idea that knowledge should be internalised to generate both a positive and permanent attitude towards changing behaviour. Jansson (1995) finds, as do many others, not only, 'simply speaking, that the better educated more easily understand the [healthy diet] information' (p. 463), but also that positive attitudes towards change are more important than education. Moreover, conservative attitudes in the division of domestic labour between men and women tend to be reproduced in dietary choice.[9] In this respect, certain attitudes towards information in general can be counterproductive. At one extreme, there can be such a belief in the scientific community and its powers that it is thought that foods would not be allowed if they were unhealthy. At the other extreme, fostered by a perceived failure to agree amongst experts, is the view that information is worthless. Cutting across these two extremes is an unrealistic optimism or fatalism – someone else will be unlucky or there is nothing I can do, respectively – and stances of superiority or inferiority – I know this already, this message is intended for somebody else who needs it, or this is beyond me.[10]

The final stage in the trickle-down of CHNT is the translation of knowledge into action. Here the literature is quite mixed. Some find a high degree of knowledge that is not acted upon,[11] others find that supermarket and other campaigns can be successful.[12] Many refer to the previously discussed issues of the inconsistency and complexity of beliefs, the changing of messages over time, the difficulty of nutritional knowledge itself and translating this into a recognisably healthy diet, the competing sources of information, and the competing demands made by food other than for health.[13]

It is precisely at the point of translating nutritional knowledge into action that other sources of knowledge than those gleaned through trickle-down become prominent. Such informal sources of knowledge are more difficult to pin down and correspond to the notion of common knowledge or commonsense. Thus, BNF, DHSS, HEC (1977) do recognise the role in nutrition education both of 'which foods are offered and how they are prepared, whether at home or at work' (p. 40 *and* of 'knowledge generated in childhood' (p. 5). But these are generally set aside in further analysis or policy prescription, although not on the basis of any apparent conviction or demonstration of their lack of importance. Implicit is the idea that such common-sense knowledge is derivative of more overt attempts at nutrition education. The neglect of the informal sources of nutrition knowledge, however, has the crucial effect of simultaneously neglecting the major influences on knowledge played by the food system itself, not in its informational activities as such, which are explicitly recognised, in advertising and labelling, but in its effects on the generation of common-sense knowledge. The food system plays a significant part in determining informal nutrition knowledge simply by virtue of the fact that it determines what foods are available. Experience of food is a direct source of knowledge; it tends to generate self-sustaining tastes and an equally supportive selection from the knowledge available to rationalise choice when this is made consciously. As Guthrie (1978, p. 58) observes:

> Practically all food behavior is learned; it is more likely, however, to be influenced by experience than by education about the merits of a food. Foods will be eaten only if they are liked. They won't be liked unless they are tasted, and they will only be tasted if they are available.[14]

But the question of food availability is given little attention in the literature. As an exception, Mooney (1990, p. 119) investigates some of the barriers to implementing health education messages effectively and concludes that 'Efforts to promote healthy eating should at every level combine nutrition education with programmes to increase the availability of cheap healthy foods.'[15] In acknowledging the importance of cost and availability of healthy food, Mooney opens the way to recognising the interaction between the food and information systems in the adoption of diet. However, there is in her own account no explanation of the reasons for the different costs and availabilities of foods, nor of the reasons why the food industry and retailers continue to promote expensive and/or unhealthy food. The implicit assumption is that liaison between government and the food industry will automatically improve diet.[16]

In contrast with some of the health education literature concentrating on the formal informational influence on food choice, other research into influences on food choice have emphasised the importance of non-informational factors. The Health Education Authority, reporting on diet amongst low-income groups, considers that for this group of consumers nutritional information has little impact on food choice: 'Major influences on people's food purchasing are not health and nutritional knowledge, but factors such as access to shops, family preferences, cooking facilities, confidence in preparing food, and income' (HEA, 1989, p. 7). Some of the non-informational barriers to healthy eating are also discussed by Sheiham (1991), who finds that lack of availability and the additional time required to prepare healthy food were not regarded as a barrier by the majority of respondents to a survey, but that the cost of healthy food, family pressure and personal taste were cited as major obstacles to change.[17]

What role is to be played by nutritional education?

The neglect of the food system even as a background source of knowledge reflects an implicit belief that consumers do or can determine the foods made available through their conscious and informed choices.[18] That this is not so emerges as soon as the issue is examined empirically in any detail. What nutritional knowledge do consumers have, where do they get it, and how do they use it?

The nutrition education literature includes assessments of the level of nutritional knowledge and evaluation of nutrition education's effectiveness in changing it: 'Thus a valid measurement of nutritional knowledge is necessary to be able to understand the relationship between nutritional knowledge, attitudes and food choice, and in order to develop and test the efficacy of nutritional interventions' (Towler and Shepherd, 1990, p. 255). This literature is usually concerned with measurement of nutritional knowledge against some criteria reflecting CHNT. It thus implicitly adopts and evaluates the trickle-down model of information provision from 'scientific truth' to consumer understanding, to be discussed later in greater depth. For example, Anderson *et al.* (1988) tested the under-standing of the principles of nutrition by a questionnaire to patients in a general medical ward. The aim of the study was to examine whether health education messages disseminated to consumers were being absorbed and, when they were, whether they were being translated into practical knowledge. The process of acquiring nutri-tional knowledge was identified as incorporating different stages: familiarity with nutritional terms, understanding principles of current nutritional recommendations, and understanding practical applications of the recommendations in terms of food purchase, preparation and eating.

There are two significant assumptions underlying this and other studies. First, there is recognition of the duality of information provision. Nutrition education competes side-by-side with, or includes, other sources of information and knowledge that are potentially misleading. But these tend to be confined to overt influences such as producer advertising that are not necessarily conducive to nutritionally sound advice and behaviour. The second assumption is that there is a direct relationship between changed nutritional knowledge and dietary choice. As suggested by Guthrie (quoted in McManus, 1990, p. 389): 'If nutrition education is to be effective, it must focus on communicating well-defined pieces of information with a goal of influencing behavior.' Although it is often recognised that influencing attitudes and knowledge does not necessarily result in changing behaviour, even in the intended direction, this remains the core motivation for nutrition education. Other influences on behaviour are perceived to be outside the prac-tical scope of nutrition education, except on some of the rare occasions when nutrition education is actually being evaluated, and much less so when it is being designed and implemented. Thus, McManus (1990, p. 389) recognises that 'Nutrition education, per se, cannot change the food supply.' This means that in the absence of an explanation of consumer behaviour encompassing a broader scope than as a result of formal information provision, there is limited understanding of how nutrition education competes with and interacts with other sources of knowledge. In short, there tends to be little discussion of ways of acquiring knowledge other than through nutrition education – except when advertising is acknowledged.

The deficiencies of these contributions, even where they begin to acknowledge wider sources of information and their interaction, can be highlighted by positing a complete inversion of the logic that they presume. Suppose that diets are fixed by factors other than information, and it is the latter which is chosen from the menu of sources made available. Nutritional knowledge is then simply the passive response to previously and otherwise determined food choices. This must, indeed, be part of the truth and the relation between the food and information systems and their implications for nutrition education might be better seen in terms of the tensions created in both the choices and the ideologies of the consumer.

A rather different illustration of these points is to be found in the commonly adopted stance that the acquisition and use of nutritional knowledge is the responsibility of the consumer, although this is subject to reservations in the regulation of what foods are permissible (for example, legislation on additives) and what (mis)information is allowed (as in labelling and advertising). These are discussed later, but, again, the account taken of the food and information systems is limited in scope. Thus, for McManus (1990, p. 393), nutrition education is concerned with: '(1) designing effective intervention strategies in a variety of settings, and (2) conducting research to determine the behavioral and health effects of the best available interventions.' As a general approach, this is unobjectionable depending upon the breadth of the scope of the 'settings'. But these are confined to supporting the consumer in the marketplace, not in relation to the content of what is to be found in the marketplace itself: 'To plan effective intervention strategies, nutrition and health-care educators must arm the consumer with skills to become effective in the marketplace' (p. 393). This view is pervasive in the labelling debate, where the provision of nutrition and health information through labelling is coupled with a need for health education for the consumer to understand and apply the information provided. Good foods and diet are presumed to follow on automatically.

They do not. Specifically, Nichols *et al.* (1988) evaluated the effectiveness of a nutritional health education leaflet in changing public knowledge and attitudes about eating and health. They suggest that the mass distribution of a leaflet promoting healthy food was not an effective method of health education. Their evidence was that the leaflet had not *increased* public knowledge of healthy eating.[19] This was partly because the survey showed a high knowledge of nutritional issues in the group that had not received the health education leaflet. This indicates a variety of other sources of information on healthy eating and begs the question of where this knowledge comes from and why it is not acted upon.[20] What this contribution demonstrates, then, is that healthy eating is not necessarily promoted by popularised information. Yet, on this basis, local food health policies (LFHPs) form a core part of health education: 'Most of these policies are based on the principle of informed choice and aim to promote dietary change by increasing levels of food availability and nutritional awareness' (Gibson *et al.*, 1990, p. 55). LFHPs are initiated locally by Health Authorities and Health Boards and are targeted to specific groups – NHS staff and patients and various groups in the community, for example. Evaluation of their effectivity is rare and, even when undertaken, is predominantly concerned with 'levels of nutritional knowledge or dietary behaviour, with little attention being paid to investigations of food availability' (Gibson *et al.*, 1990, p. 55).

Once the most informal, but potentially most influential, sources of food information have been set aside, attention shifts to a perceived duality within formal sources of nutrition education – comprised of those which are specifically, and possibly exclusively, concerned with it and those, such as commercial organisations within the food system, which are bound by objectives other than nutritional health for the nation. The division between these two sources is made up of a number of aspects. Each is bound to channels of communication with different origins, destinations and with a differing content of information to be disseminated. Health educators derive their information primarily from expert committees and scientific research; their closest links are with government. Commercial organisations might also have some such links but they are primarily governed by market research and product development. They communicate through advertising, packaging, labelling and, ultimately, use and habituation. Driven by the imperatives of profitability, whatever nutritional information is supplied is necessarily mixed with, and usually dominated by, other inducements to purchase and consume.

The separation between these two sources of information is, however, not so clear-cut. Government intervenes to regulate advertising and labelling standards, partly in response to the food industry's use of government's nutrition education as an advertising ploy, as in health claims for products. On the other hand, commercially produced leaflets relating to health and nutrition form a large part (59 per cent) of those available in one district health authority. This is due to several factors: insufficient funding for health authorities to provide their own leaflets coupled with a perceived need to provide such information somehow; and the willingness of the food industry to provide information which can provide an opportunity at least for a public relations exercise if not necessarily for direct product endorsement. More generally, Sanderson and Winkler (1983, p. 1353) report: 'Even in schools educational materials from the HEC [Health Education Council] are outweighed by the "study kits" provided by companies.' Whatever the merits of commercial sponsorship in general, the recent trend towards its use in nutrition education seems less acceptable when coming from the food industry than were the latter to direct its support to sport or the arts in which there is less of a direct commercial interest.

This has raised a debate over the benefits of collaboration between health educators and the food industry. For some, the food industry is the best communicator, at the front line, as it were, as food purchases are being made. For Guthrie (1978, p. 58):

> We must use the techniques that have been used success-fully in communicating. Let's use the expertise of the journalist, the educators, and the media specialist. Tell them what to say, but let them show us how to say it.

She recognises, however, that the provision of healthy eating information and healthy product options may still conflict with nutrition education in that

> there is a limit to what we can learn from advertisers because we want to promote diversity, substitution rather than brand loyalty, and moderation rather than quantity . . . it is much easier to add a habit which provides some immediate satisfactions than it is to eliminate or modify one whose unfavourable consequences are remote . . . as long as food, especially high-calorie food, tastes good, we will have problems with people who eat too much.
>
> (p. 58)

Perhaps this is why the food industry is content to be seen to collaborate with health educators; healthy products are an additional product, not necessarily a substitution for the highly processed and high value-added food which continues to be sold.

Those who adopt a favourable stance on the potential use of commercial sources of nutrition also tend to view the food industry as responsive to consumer demand. Following the NACNE and

COMA reports, healthy eating became newsworthy and is perceived to have correspondingly shifted consumer demand. Slattery (1986) reviews the developments in the UK food industry following the NACNE and COMA reports, describing the activities of manufacturers and retailers. According to her, minimal industry response will occur if confined to production and promotion of the currently available food supply rather than significantly changing it. The notion of 'healthy food' becomes one that is more in line with COMA recommendations. Thus, foods with any healthy attribute begin to be marketed as such: 'Manufacturers of a product which already has clear health attributes may begin to use "healthiness" in promoting the product, without altering the food in any way' (Slattery, 1986, p. 6). For example, the need to reduce fat consumption stressed in the COMA report has been taken up by the food industry to promote margarine with a high polyunsaturated fat content: '87% of those questioned by Food Policy Research agreed that 'polyunsaturated fat is better for you than saturated fat'. It is unlikely that the health education council would have achieved this without the power of Van den Bergh's purse' (Fallows and Gosden, 1985, p. 15). Fallows and Gosden point out that Van den Bergh and Jurgens brands account for 50 per cent of total UK margarine production and for £12 million p.a. in promotion, far above the resources available to the health educators. In addition, they suggest that consumer understanding of the foods which are a major source of fibre reflects advantage taken by food manufacturers in promoting their products as sources of fibre: bread was mentioned by 75 per cent of consumers as a source of fibre, breakfast cereals by 60 per cent, but potatoes and pulses by only 18 per cent and 8 per cent of consumers, respectively.[21]

On the basis of their research, Fallows and Gosden conclude that publications such as COMA and NACNE, and the media attention they receive, have an impact on public attitudes, knowledge and behaviour, and solicit a food industry response. No one doubts the presence of these channels of communication and influence but they do have to be balanced against the role of other, continuing determinants of the production and consumption of unhealthy foods. These do not seem to be recognised as a barrier to the eventual take up of dietary recommendations: 'We are convinced that nutrition is having an increasing impact as a determinant of food choice, and this impact is likely to accelerate as the nutrition educators' message is reinforced through product development and marketing effort' (Fallows and Gosden, 1985, p. 46).

In contrast to healthy margarines, foods containing ingredients which have been associated with health risks have been marketed in ways to draw attention away from this. A more positive response is the removal or addition of ingredients according to their healthiness. Nonetheless, producers are seen as making limited changes in deference to this. Slattery (1986, p. 17) observes the

> growing popularity of 'naturalness', leading to many new products claiming to be 'free from: added preservatives, colours, flavourings or sugar or salt'. This has meant the appearance of the 'does not contain' label next to the 'contents' label. Such developments may do little for the public image of the whole industry since the traditional products continue in production – often from the same manufacturer.[22]

This contrasts with the response of retailers who are identified as having a commitment towards the provision of 'healthier' foods. This is based on moves towards nutritional labelling, in a growing range of 'healthy' own-label foods, and the stocking of more branded 'healthy' foods and the provision of information and promotion material geared to healthy eating. The retailers surveyed by Slattery were the large supermarket chains, but no mention is made of the cost of 'healthy' food. It is implied that the perceived increase in healthy eating is being adequately responded to by retailers:

> From the information supplied by all retailers, it is clear that serious consideration is being taken of current health issues and retailers are evidently prepared for the effect that health concerns will have on food choice in the future.
>
> (Slattery, 1986, p. 128)

In contrast, a more critical interpretation of the contribution of the commercial part of the food system to nutrition education is offered by Lobstein (1990), who cites evidence from April Brett's investigation of nutrition education leaflets used in a district health authority. The extent of the infiltration of commercially produced leaflets is particularly marked in the provision of information around baby and infant feeding. This information is actively sought by parents. Lobstein argues that information presented in this way by commercial organisations can mislead by omission of information; by emphasis on only some aspects, such as ease of preparation and benefits of convenience foods; by attempting to create scientific legitimation for products; and by emphasising particular brand names instead of groups of food types.

For Lobstein, one of the effects of such developments may well be to impair the separation between the two sources of information, conflating commercially and non-commercially motivated education. McCluney (1988), for example, finds that GPs and Health Centres were the preferred source of advice on diet for 87 per cent of survey respondents, although only 23 per cent of respondents had ever received information in this way.[23] Lobstein (1990, p. 23) warns: 'Clients of the service may start to see clinics and health professionals as mere extensions of the food industry.' His article implies that the profit imperatives of the food industry make it virtually impossible for the necessary unbiased, accurate information to be provided by them but, in the absence of any other alternative, this commercially produced material is what people seeking information from health authority clinics are getting. Thus, there is a danger that commercially produced information is endorsed because it is supplied through health professionals, or that the health professionals' credibility is reduced because of the content and source of the health information when commercially sourced.[24] Possibly the fear is that non-commercially oriented information and sources will become as devalued as food advertisements which are generally viewed with scepticism[25] (although this does not necessarily mean they are ineffective).

At times, this leads to the extreme position that commercial and non-commercial sources of nutrition education should be fully separated from one another by the simple expedient of preventing the former from participating altogether. This is so for those who seek to prevent the food industry from using health claims. Harper (1989), for example, recognises that such claims are commercially and possibly politically motivated, that they are specific to individual products whereas disease and diet are multifaceted, and health claims are necessarily made in simplified, and potentially false, forms without qualification. Campbell and O'Connor (1988) concur, 'given the unlikely possibility that a single nutrient effect will be demonstrated in a clinical trial' (p. 90), so that health claims will be scientifically inaccurate, and will only be of short-term benefit as all competitors follow suit, thereby diminishing consumer interest in information. They also point to a regulatory nightmare in allowing health claims in adverts, as they would have to be screened and are not subject to easy verification or refutation. They conclude that 'no claims of any kind should be placed on food container labels' because of 'depreciation in scientific research credibility', and doubt whether it would be even in the long-term economic interests of the food industry (p. 91).

Both Harper and Campbell and O'Connor are sharply aware of the impossibility of translating scientific information into commercial health claims. This leads them to wish to prohibit them altogether but without their having examined the implications of and for other determinants of food choice.[26] This reflects a wish to keep the laboratory out of the marketplace. In addition, because of the perceived impossibility of communicating appropriate information, Campbell and O'Connor interestingly adopt a model in which information through health claims is eventually ineffective over the long term and an unnecessary cost and disadvantage to the food industry. This contrasts with the unfolding theory to be discussed below in which good information can be disseminated and become a permanent feature of product advertising.

Thus, those who object to health claims tend to employ the same theory as those who do not but are cynical about health claims as a positive source of education. Each side, as will be demonstrated, neglects other influences on food choice.

The good, the bad, the commercial and the non-commercial

Whilst much of the previous section has been concerned with the contributions of those who are active in nutrition education, some adopt an explicit *theoretical* approach, even if others only employ an implicit analytical framework. In each case, all tend to be wedded to what will be termed a 'double duality'. The first duality is between the *providers* of information, those who genuinely seek to serve consumers through nutritional information, addressing advertising and labelling regulation, and so on, as opposed to those in the commercial world whose primary objective is to make profits. The second duality is across the information itself, between whether it is good or bad in determining diet. This might be close to true or false by the criterion of CHNT but, as has been seen, food knowledge and action do not necessarily fall so easily into such simple categories. Indeed, the same is true of good and bad in so far as what might be good for a marginal change in diet for one food might be bad for others – as in 'lite' products which can encourage complementary consumption of heavy products rather than substituting for them: a sugarless diet coke justifies a fatty bag of chips.

The crucial theoretical point about the double duality is that the two need not correspond to one another.[27] If they do, there is little of analytical interest, although a fierce practical struggle may be in prospect. Commerce must be prevented from promoting unhealthy diet through bad information, although there might be some residual defence offered on the grounds either that consumers should have the freedom to be duped or that competition will ultimately eliminate those products that are unhealthy even if they temporarily survive through malicious advertising. The latter case, the 'unfolding process' of superior products *and* 'good' information, will be covered later.

Setting aside the extreme case in which the dualities coincide, and also leaving aside, not entirely realistically, the issue of whether non-commercial sources of information are unambiguously committed to good information, then concern is with the extent to which commercial interests are wedded to good as opposed to bad information. In short, it is a matter of how educators and commerce interact with one another to provide for better or worse information and, possibly, better or worse products as consumers act upon information provided. In yet other words, can educators work through the commercial system, and, if so, what is the most fruitful way? And are educators and commerce fundamentally in conflict with one another or are they in symbiosis?

One implicit way of acknowledging these problems is through 'social marketing' – a suggestion that nutritional education should be both like commerce (marketing) and not so (social rather than profit-oriented). The attempt has been made by Lefebvre *et al.* (1995) to 'sell' social marketing for nutritional education. Little more is involved than a socially responsible extension of commercial marketing and its techniques where nutritional goals are substituted for those of profitability, at least in the realm of purchasing:

> Social marketing is concerned with introducing and disseminating new ideas and issues and increasing the prevalence of specific behavior among target groups. . . . Social marketing has its roots in marketing theory, which, in turn, is primarily based on theories of consumer behavior (exchange theory being one example).
>
> (p. 146)

As van den Heede and Pelican (1995) observe, referring to the work of Habermas, this involves a particular view about education that is open to question by appealing to a broader notion of developing individual capacities and autonomy than would be suggested by the use of marketing techniques. What is notably absent, however, from both contributions is discussion of power and its specific content in the context of food. For Lefebvre *et al.* (1995), social marketing is the best way to change people and their behaviour, however much this might be disguised as something else to make it appear more acceptable:[28]

> As a planning system, social marketing incorporates an understanding of, or theory about, how people make behavior choices and then folds that understanding into program development. Examples of such theories include the stages of change model, the health belief model, social learning theory, diffusion of innovations, and several models that focus on community organizations and social planning.
>
> (p. 147)

Quite apart from the status of such eclectic theoretical fragments in understanding how people change, vanden Heede and Pelican (1995) express an appropriate concern over the failure to distinguish marketing, social or otherwise, from education in a number of ways – that education should be interactive not disseminative, developmental and not manipulative, convey meaning not messages, and be critical and ethical in scope and not consumer-oriented.

Significantly, this dispute has nothing to do with food as such, even if nutritional education is its chosen battleground. It does, however, incorporate a common theme across the literature – that commerce has the *advantage* in communicating information. This is thought to be so for three separate reasons. The first, as in the social marketing debate, is because it has experience in marketing techniques and, consequently, these should be emulated by those without commercial orientation. Second, commerce is in day-to-day contact with consumers by virtue of the products that are sold. Whether in advertising or labels, they are communicating, at the front line as it were, both in terms of frequency of contact, at least as often as purchase itself, and in a form that corresponds to the complex and immediate meanings of foods rather than the more esoteric nutritional advice. Third, commerce has the secure capacity to finance provision of information, whether in advertising or packaging, often as a complement to, rather than as a drag upon, its pursuit of profitability. For Ippolito and Mathios (1994a, p. 202), for example:

> In contrast to government and general sources of information, producer-provided information is unlikely to contain generic information about food categories and is less likely to provide broad guidance on dietary choices. Instead, producer-provided information is typically focused on a particular food, identifying where the brand is superior to its competitors and why the consumer should consider this difference important enough to buy the product. . . . Also, producer-provided information may be more prominent to many consumers because of the increased quantity of claims and the different mix of media used for making the claims.

It follows that commerce is better placed, rather than better as such, to provide food information by its experience, its location in the food chain, and in the availability of finance. Indeed, the competitive mechanism will have guaranteed a degree of success across each of these aspects of advantage, otherwise the products concerned will have failed. Consequently, the presence of food information will have evolved along with the advertising, products and commercial success of the food industry itself, with the survival of the fittest to the fore.

Collaboration between nutritionists and commerce?[29]

Of course, this does not necessarily entail that commercial sources of food knowledge are either good or bad simply because they have an evolved advantage in some respects over alternative sources of information. As already seen, it can be argued, precisely because of these advantages, that the food industry should be totally disbarred from providing health claims. Nonetheless, not surprisingly, there is the temptation to emulate the food industry, as in use of social marketing, or to work through it because of its greater informational purchase on the consumer.

This is the position adopted by Kirk (1991). He takes as his starting point the increasing use of nutrition and health information in food marketing. He concludes that this warrants collaboration between dietitians and the food industry so that such information is provided more beneficially from an educational perspective.[30] The core of the argument is that nutritional knowledge of particular products is primarily obtained through labelling which is signalled by (health claim) advertising. Historically, this begs the question of why nutritional health should have assumed a greater prominence over the recent period and, consequently, why the food and information systems should not already have been interacting satisfactorily for consumers. For, otherwise, it is far from clear why dietitians would be a sufficient (or, indeed, a positive) corrective. The absence of consideration of these broader issues, even as background, is associated with a further narrowing of the set of more immediate and relevant factors that are taken into account.

First, labelling and advertising tend to be seen in isolation from, and independent of, other sources of information about food and the other practices of purchasing, preparing and consuming it:

> Nutrition labelling should be considered of central importance to nutrition education because, despite any shortcomings, nutrition labelling is the main method whereby the consumer can assess the nutrient profile of food. . . . Consumers can use nutrition labelling and nutrition claims on labels in the supermarket *at the time of food purchase* to help them evaluate and compare foods in order to make healthy food choices. Leisurely examination at home of the nutrition information given on the food-label can help future purchase decisions.
>
> (Kirk, 1991, p. 198)

Beyond this, other determinants of food choice are notable for their absence. Indeed, there appears to be a presumption that the major issue concerns *change* in CHNT or product lines rather than an accumulated and continuing deficiency in the nation's diet (and knowledge). Thus, the problems of labelling in the past are associated with the lag in response to the shift in CHNT away from focus on proteins, vitamins and minerals, and towards reducing fats, sugar and salt and increasing fibre. And the consumer is perceived to depend upon labelling to cope with 'a nutritionally modified product bearing a nutritional claim instead of a standard product' (Kirk, 1991, p. 198). The presumption is that the standard product is already being handled satisfactorily by the consumer but that problems arise out of products suddenly becoming 'nutritionally modified' where previously they were standard.

The focus on advertising and labelling also has the effect of placing the emphasis on individual products rather than on diet as a whole, although this is a further reflection of the implicit belief that broad nutritional education is already satisfactory. To be explicit, promoting specific products through advertising and labelling their relative healthiness may lead to overeating as 'good' foods complement rather than substitute for the 'bad'. One response of the meat industry in the UK to the growing concern over levels of fat consumption is to advertise the health of lean meat as a food. The intention of jumping onto the health bandwagon may well have the impact of sustaining the consumption of all meats. The symbiotic relation between dietitians and the food industry, sought for by Kirk, promises much less potential once the focus shifts away from promoting the nutritionally healthy (on which both sides can collaborate to promote a new product, for example) and towards reducing the unhealthy and overall levels of consumption, to which producers may be vehemently opposed. This points to the contradiction between producers, who seek to sell particular products, and dietitians, who should be concerned with diet as a whole.

Kirk rehearses a number of arguments that have been employed against use of health claims in advertising and products. He finds it necessary to address these in order to sustain his view that dietitians should promote such claims in collaboration with the food industry. Thus, he considers the ethics of food claims (use of the fear of disease), uncertainty of evidence, the potential exaggerated impact on health of specific foods, diet as a potentially damaging self-medication, the devaluation of nutritional information, and potential bias in research towards substantiating product claims as opposed to more fundamental research. His arguments here are not so much wrong as distorted in emphasis, partly reflecting a wish to maintain professional standards amongst dietitians but, more seriously, revealing an uncritical attitude to what faces the profession in the form of the continuing food and information systems. On ethics, for example, the issue of professional standards amongst dietitians must surely be set against the total lack of compunction displayed by advertising in marketing products – where all the vices and virtues are recruited to promote a sale. Similarly, the question of research bias has to be seen against the limited budgets available relative to those employed by food processors to enhance profitability independently of nutritional content.

In short, Kirk appears to adopt a naive view of the extent to which, and the way in which, dietitians might engage collaboratively with the food industry. Quite apart from the relative strength of the two parties, there is a complete neglect of the different levels at which the food and information systems operate and the extent to which the food industry has a presence at, and influence over, all of them. The strategic choice for dietitians might be better served by the image of a slingless David versus a stone-holding Goliath than of junior, but respected partner!

The unfolding of healthy eating

Although not directly concerned with collaboration between dietitians and the food industry, a more formal and theoretically informed stance comparable to that of Kirk is taken by Ippolito and Mathios (1990, 1993, 1994a, 1994b, 1995) in a series of articles.[31] They wish to see restrictions lifted on health claims in food advertising.[32] Their work has two components – one theoretical and the other empirical. Theoretically, they recognise that, in pursuit of profitability, the food industry might deploy either truthful or deceptive advertising, itself an oversimplified notion of food knowledge. Their predilection, however, is towards believing that truthful information would tend to predominate and proliferate:[33]

> From an economic perspective, there are important theoretical reasons to believe that a policy of allowing a broader range of truthful diet–disease claims would be beneficial, because this policy would increase the opportunity, and thus the competitive pressure on firms, to market the nutritional features of food effectively. Also, if producer claims are an important source of information for many consumers, a greater freedom to make valid claims could spread the information more effectively to allow a larger portion of the population to improve more of their dietary decisions. Whether the competitive process and normal deception policy were adequate to fill in missing information and control deception is, of course, open to question and empirical testing.
>
> (Ippolito and Mathios, 1994a, p. 201)

The reason for this inversion of Gresham's Law for money – that the bad drives the good out of circulation – is because of the theory of 'unfolding'. Because consumers are interested in food information, those products without information will be out-competed in the marketplace. Exactly the same applies to competition between products with good and bad information. Ultimately, consumers will settle upon the former, with both healthy products and truthful information prevailing. However, should health claims be banned altogether, there is no possibility for this unfolding process to materialise, and commerce will concentrate on products, and information to sell them, that have a different orientation than healthy/unhealthy. The result is a missed opportunity to employ the commercial advantage in disseminating food information and, thereby, to improve food choice from existing products as well as inducing healthier products themselves:

> Consumers . . . can switch from foods they are currently eating to the healthiest foods available. . . . Second, consumers can switch to more healthful versions of the foods they are currently eating . . . [as] many consumers are unlikely to give up their favorite types of foods to improve their diets, then information related to healthier versions of those favorite foods may prove especially important.
>
> (Ippolito and Mathios, 1993, p. 188)

These presumptions have been contested. As Schucker *et al.* (1992, p. 79) observe, the compulsion to board the health bandwagon may not always be on the basis of a valid ticket:

> products with a large number of flagged nutrient characteristics gain market share while competitive products with fewer flagged nutrients lose. . . . A disquieting implication . . . is that such labeling may have the potential to exaggerate nutritional differences between products and lead to horsepower races between competitors . . . without regard to the quality or health relevance of the nutrients being featured.

Further, Nestle (1994) has argued that one of the consequences of the ideological shift towards healthy eating has been that traditionally healthy diets, such as the Mediterranean, Japanese and Native Hawaiian, have been appropriated for mass production and advertising, and their nutritional content compromised.[34]
More generally, there are three main weaknesses with the

theoretical account of Ippolito and Mathios. First, the food information system is simply conceived, as outlined before, in terms of a double duality – good and bad information from commercial and non-commercial sources, if not respectively. There is no recognition of the complexity of food information, the variety of sources and meanings, and how these are translated into action.[35]

Consider, for example, the role of advertising on children's breakfast-time television. The extent of such advertising has been deplored, along with the time that children spend watching TV at the expense of other activities.[36] Such advertising has been associated with eating problems and with the sale of unhealthy foods. Most instructive is the contrast between the US Food Guide Pyramid and the Saturday Morning Advertising Pyramid (Figure 4.1) which shows the difference in proportions between a balanced diet and the weight of advertising to children. Ironically then, as Hill (1995) observes, even though cereals are, subject to what is added to them, a good food, they are often perceived negatively by adults since they are heavily advertised with children as targets. Thus, advertising to promote a healthy food can create an opposite effect.

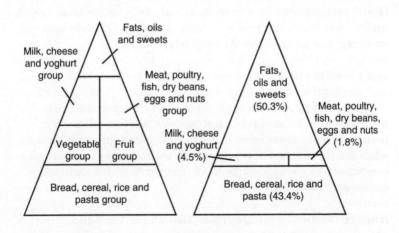

Figure 4.1 The unhidden persuaders: US Food Guide Pyramid (left) and Saturday Morning Advertising Pyramid (right)

Source: Kotz and Story (1994, p. 1299).

A second weakness of the approach of Ippolito and Mathios is that the food system is also simply conceived. It is reduced to the pursuit of profitability through varying the mixture of products made available and the information attached to them. Accordingly, dramatic changes in agriculture, food processing, retailing, eating habits, domestic technology, and household lifestyles and meal habits, and so on, are overlooked. Innovation in the provision of food only originates with the scientific community in its CHNT, even if it is filtered through commerce.

Third, the interaction between the food and food information systems is confined to the unfolding process. This is successful or not depending upon government regulations and the relative merits for profits of truth and deception. But the impact of unfolding is necessarily confined to the impact upon individual products taken one at a time. Indeed, this is precisely the direction taken by Ippolito and Mathios in their empirical work, attempting to show dietary improvement across a range of products between 1985 and 1990 when a window of opportunity was temporarily opened, but then closed again, by a weakening of US regulations on advertising, labelling and health claims. However, the impact upon *overall* diet and health is much more complex. The proliferation of diet and health products has both encouraged the pressures to eat *more* because of the wider choices available and as a reward for choosing a healthy product and to eat *less* in the attempt to match ideals of health and beauty. The result, as discussed in Chapter 3, has been to encourage eating disorders. More generally, the working of the food and food information systems cannot be legitimately reduced, even as a first approximation, to the unfolding or not of healthy foods and legitimate health claims.

The empirical evidence presented by Ippolito and Mathios is no more satisfactory. Essentially, they seek to show that shifts towards a healthier diet accelerated and broadened in the period 1985–90, when restrictions on health claims were eased. Consequently, they conclude that, whilst admitting government health messages in the earlier period had some effect, they were much more effectively communicated by manufacturing, advertising, and so on, across a range of products, especially those harder to identify directly with nutritional advice, and across a range of socioeconomic groups, especially those hard to educate.

One weakness of Ippolito and Mathios's empirical work, which they acknowledge, is the failure to address their hypothesis or, more exactly, their hypotheses, *directly*.[37] They can only claim that

> These results are consistent with the hypothesis that producer-provided information is likely to be effective across a broader range of food categories, so that in the presence of other sources of information, improvements will occur more rapidly.
>
> (Ippolito and Matthias, 1994a, p. 215)

As advertising using health messages is adjudged to have been causal, it should have been used as an explanatory variable. Although some informal evidence is presented of the use of health claims to promote products, data do not exist to undertake statistical tests of their significance. The second claim is as follows:

> The evidence is not consistent with the alternative hypothesis that the change in policy in 1985, which allowed producer health claims under the general deception rules for advertising, undermined public health efforts to provide information leading to better dietary choices.
>
> (Ippolito and Mathias, 1994a, p. 216)

However, no evidence is presented, not even informal, on whether deceptive gave way to valid advertising. Wallace *et al.* (1993), for example, find increasing market health claims in a study of advertising in four women's magazines over the entire period from 1975 to 1990. They reasonably ask whether this is capitalising upon or promoting awareness of a healthy diet. Their evidence is consistent with the hypothesis that advertising did not change more favourably in line with product changes. In any case, even if there is a significantly different positive change towards healthy eating behaviour between 1985 and 1990, this might be due to any number of causes other than health claims as such. In addition, the appeal to healthy eating ads or labels is far from convincing since the use of false health claims and images remained endemic. It could as well be argued that consumers' reaction against all commercial health claims led them more readily to heed earlier and continuing government advice.

A second weakness of the empirical work is the use of timing. Even by their own account, Ippolito and Mathios recognise the potential for commerce to go off in the direction of competitive false claims rather than to compete to be truthful. Consequently, the *prior* restrictions on health claims and reliance upon officially sanctioned advice may have been important in foreclosing the path of deceptive claims. Further, the continuing vigilance over advertising and even fear of the reimposition of restrictions is arguably essential to pre-empt future cumulative competitions in deception.

Finally, the issue of timing is important in assessing Ippolito and Mathios's claims purely in a statistical sense. They do credit non-commercial dietary advice with having initiated the move towards some healthier eating patterns. Simple patterns of diffusion would suggest that such a process would accelerate across the population from slow beginnings as, for example, individuals learn from one another. Consequently, Ippolito and Mathios might be measuring a typical diffusion process with the most rapid period of change coinciding by chance with the period of looser advertising restrictions. Certainly, the alternative that is implied, in the absence of other interventions, of even spread of knowledge over time, irrespective of the numbers who have already learnt, is unacceptable. The more who know, the more there are to do the telling but the fewer still to be told. Ironically, if typical diffusion is involved, then we can already anticipate future articles by Ippolito and Mathios deploring the reimposition of restrictions on health claims because of the decline in the pace of adopting healthy eating. Possibly, again by chance, the diffusion effect will already have begun to have tailed off!

Interestingly, other empirical tests used by Ippolito and Mathios point to anomalous statistical techniques. They run regressions on per capita consumption of various foods on time and with a dummy for the period 1985–90, finding greater negative trends for some unhealthy foods and greater positive trends for some healthy foods in the period of looser health claim restrictions (Ippolito and Mathios, 1995). Unfortunately, the implication of their statistics is that per capita consumption of healthy foods will grow indefinitely and those of unhealthy foods will shrink to zero in finite time and even become negative!

From a purely statistical point of view, then, as in the earlier discussion of diffusion, this suggests that Ippolito and Mathios's tests are entirely inappropriate, and the issue of timing, even excluding the effect of other factors, has been carelessly treated. Further, casual evidence from other countries that similar processes were at work, but in the absence of the USA's particular regulatory history, as in the adoption of skimmed milks for example,[38] casts doubt on their hypotheses. Significantly, they do not seem to be aware of the potential to employ comparative evidence.[39]

Towards an alternative

In many ways, this empirical commentary lies within the analytical framework adopted by Ippolito and Mathios. Our intention, however, has been to launch a much broader theoretical critique. It has the following components. The trickle-down understanding of food information must be rejected for a number of reasons. The simple division between true or false knowledge is inappropriate, as is the idea of the commercial and non-commercial as the exclusive sources of knowledge. Knowledge is gained from day-to-day experience of food. The complexity of food knowledge and the variety of meanings and roles occupied by foods imply that there is no simple translation of knowledge into action.

In short, a more satisfactory starting point for examining the role of knowledge in determining eating habits is in studying the food and food information systems and their interaction. In some respects, despite itself, this is the direction in which much of the literature has pointed. It takes for granted, for example, an existing knowledge and set of eating habits upon which trickle-down of CHNT is supposed to do its work. But we need to know how eating knowledge has arisen before accommodating changes in it and its effects on food choice. As observed, even for Ippolito and Mathios, the role of profitability is crucial in determining what information is disseminated in conjunction with what, potentially innovative, products. In a sense, we are asking for more of the same – a broader understanding of knowledge itself and of its sources, how these are dependent upon the food system's pursuit of profitability, which goes far beyond product innovation to promote or respond to health claims, and how these all interact with one another.

Unfortunately, within the field of nutritional education, only extremely limited progress has been made along these lines. This is primarily because of the failure to employ theory in the understanding of what nutritional education is and how it has an effect. By default, the provision of information tends to be seen as automatically leading to progress, with effectivity depending upon the content and method of disseminating the information. As Gillespie and Brun (1992, p. 223) put it in a retrospective celebration of twenty-five years of the Society for Nutrition Education: 'Most nutritionists, educators, and consumers, even if they've never read an article on nutrition education or practiced in the field, have their own theory of how nutrition education could or should influence nutrition practice.' They also observe that in 1979 an open challenge was laid down to 'develop an explicit theoretical base for nutrition education research'. Yet Achterberg and Clark (1992) find that only 25 per cent of studies in the field use theory to select variables, methods or interpret results.[40] Further, Axelson and Brinberg (1992) find that the measured relationship between nutritional knowledge and dietary behaviour has been profoundly disappointing but suggest that this is not because the relationship does not exist. Rather, it has been under-measured for having been improperly specified.

Only occasionally have there been attempts to deepen the theory of nutritional education. French and Adams (1986) seek a synthesis between three separate approaches, organised hierarchically, although their proposal is for health education more generally. At the top of the hierarchy is the model of collective action, pitched at the level of broad socioeconomic determinants. A self-empowerment model is located at an intermediate level in order to endow individuals with the capacity to determine their own lives even if within the constraints identified by the model of collective action. Finally, the lowest placed model is one of behavioural change through health education, which is seen as particularly ineffective on empirical grounds and in view of the insights offered by the more lofty models:

> The three models of health education proposed are set out in a hierarchy, because we believe that the most significant determinant of health is social and economic circumstance, and the least important individual health behaviour. This assertion is backed by a wealth of evidence, linking health status to issues such as poverty, employment, low income, and social class. We place self-empowerment next in our hierarchy because we believe that personal, psychological well-being is the next most important determinant of health status. In addition, self-empowerment approaches to health education are also ethically more justifiable. . . . Finally, we place behavioural change methods of health education at the bottom of our hierarchy . . . there is growing evidence to contradict the assumption that individual behaviour is the primary determinant of health status.
>
> (p. 73)

Rennie (1995) replicates and refines such a scheme to discuss health education in the context of food hygiene. More sophisticated approaches are to be found amongst those who have addressed food issues from a social science perspective. Bordo (1993, p. 165), for example, in her study of female eating disorders, appeals in following Foucault to 'the primacy of practice over belief. Not chiefly through ideology, but through the organisation and regulation of the time, space, and movements of our daily lives.' Not surprisingly, of the little social theory that has been applied to food knowledge, with the exception of anthropology, where the meaning of food and its rituals have been paramount, there has been an inclination to argue by analogy with medical knowledge and/or the control or construction of the body.

It is not our intention to review this literature and explore it for its potential to provide a more satisfactory account of the nature, content and impact of food knowledge. Rather, whilst it does have considerable advantages in adopting a serious analytical stance towards the questions of what constitutes knowledge and how it relates to social relations, especially those of power and empowerment, the residual weakness remains of not having incorporated the specificity of food. Eating is neither health nor sexuality, although it has connections with each. It is for this reason that it must be insisted that study of the food information system must be integrated with study of the food system itself. Only then can we hope to understand the source of the knowledge that we gain through the processes leading to eating itself and how these generate the circumstances, however indirectly and misleadingly, in which we form our knowledge and act upon it.

In this light, particularly in the context of nutritional advice and campaigning through leaflets, labelling and advertising, and so on, a more promising approach to the study of the food information system is to be found in media studies, particularly when it is applied to consumption. Surprisingly, this potential source of theory for nutritional education appears to have been entirely overlooked. In the review of media studies and consumption provided by Morley (1995), he shows how media studies was previously based on two traditions: first, there was the idea of the power and control of the media, exerted over a relatively defenceless and passive audience which was, consequently, duped and manipulated; second, there was the notion of audience resistance and its capacity to interpret the message actively and heterogeneously. The literature no longer seeks to sit at one or other of these two extremes or to strike a balance between them. Rather, a more sophisticated understanding of the media is advanced, one in which messages have to be *encoded* by those communicating and decoded by those interpreting, a more sophisticated way of handling the trickle-down of CHNT that has been outlined previously, for example.

Further, it is no longer a case of the all-powerful media, giving way to the all-powerful consumer as the latter is free to interpret at will and, as in some arguments, through an increasingly diverse choice of media, made available through information revolution. As Morley (1995, p. 309) observes:

> The problem here is that many of these arguments run the danger of abstracting these technologies' intrinsic 'capacities' from the social contexts of their actual use. In understanding such technological developments, we could more usefully follow . . . concern with the question of how these technologies are integrated into the structure and routines of domestic life.

At a general level, this is precisely what has been more particularly argued in seeking an analytical integration between the food system (loosely the social context, leading to and incorporating the routines of domestic life) and the food information system (the apparatus for delivering food knowledge, including that part of the media with that explicit purpose). Consequently, the processes of encoding/decoding, the active participation by both communicators and audience, do not take place in a vacuum but are tied to specific food and food information systems which necessarily need to be unravelled. As Morley also observes, there may be 'preferred readings' on the part of the communicator but there is no guarantee that these are taken up either as readings or in action by the various members of the audience. It needs to be added, however, that there are a variety of preferred readings, and these can be in conflict with one another and/or in conflict with preferred actions. Commercial pressures to encourage purchase of unhealthy foods may conflict with health messages, and unhealthy foods may be advertised as healthy. This returns us to old problems even if our understanding of them is considerably more advanced in terms of the nature of knowledge and how it is generated, communicated and acted upon.

Concluding remarks

By taking a more sophisticated approach to food information and the processes by which it is generated and deployed, the conventional wisdom attached to the double duality of commerce versus non-commerce as sources of knowledge, and of knowledge as true or false, disintegrates. In any case, commerce is itself extremely active in intervening to provide non-commercial sources of information. It seeks representation all the way along the food information system, funding nutritional research and forming and serving upon advisory bodies, and so on.

This, apart from serving as a guardian of its interests, is an admission that the provision and marketing of foods is not necessarily the most effective form of delivering information, even though it is so pervasive and despite this assumption on the part of those who seek to work through the commercial system rather than to constrain it. For consumer groups and the media can have an enormous impact despite, even because of, their limited resources – not least because they are more liable to be trusted. Consequently, the attitude to 'food activists' is often to treat them as troublemakers, publicity seekers and prone to exaggeration, in some respects a compliment to their effectiveness.[41] They are to nutritional education as patent medicines are to scientific healing. These accusations are not necessarily totally inaccurate, even if they are intended pejoratively.

Consider, for example, the claim of Gormley et al. (1987), who, despite their more than usually complex understanding of the food and information systems, seem to deplore the role of a minority of consumers and newsworthiness in promoting to the fore what are not necessarily the most significant sources of poorer food:

> For some time it has been apparent that the attitudes of a minority of consumers and the content of press comments on the relative risks in the diet have tended to reverse the generally accepted risk priorities. The actual order of importance of risks has been estimated to be first those due to microbiological contamination and nutritional imbalance, then (one thousandfold less) those due to environmental pollutants, contaminants, and natural toxicants, then (one hundredfold less again) those due to pesticide residues and food additives. The more extreme consumer and press comments have tended to make food

additives, pesticide residues, and environmental contami-
nants the top priorities.

(pp. 215–16)

Yet, given the determinants of food choice and nutritional knowledge, and the relative resources available to those campaigning for
an improved diet, it is more than reasonable for them to pursue
those issues on which they can gain an effective presence and as part
of a strategy to broach other issues also, even if possibly more fundamental but less prominent.

Notable is the use of terms such as 'extreme' to describe some
consumer and press comment. This might reflect the lack of
veracity of such interventions by the standards of scientific
thinking, but the appropriate comparison is more with the weight
of informational determinants of food choice that derive from the
food system more generally. Here the claims are not so much
extreme as, literally, fantastic, with the vast majority of advertised
inducements to consume bearing no relation to reality at all. This is
set aside, however, in pointing to what is perceived to be scaremon-
gering by non-commercial food activists, whether through the press
or campaigning. Essentially, actual or potential effectiveness is
being dismissed as irresponsibility. The preferred alternative, even
of those wary of the pernicious influence of commerce, is one of
cautious dissemination of securely founded CHNT through education and labelling. This is itself seen as threatened by the
sensationalism and premature publicity associated with the media,
which might also give rise to consumer confusion and loss of credibility of sound advice and information in deference to more extreme
informational interventions.[42]

Thus, Wiseman (1990, p. 399) graciously concedes that 'pressure
groups are not necessarily, as the term might imply, irresponsible
"activists" but often comprise a number of highly eminent and
responsible members of the scientific community'. Wright (1990,
p. 80), in discussing how the marketing ploy of claiming no additives has strengthened the antipathy to additives and interest in
healthier food, quotes revealingly from the chairman of the Food
and Drink Federation, p. 80:

It is all too easy to forget, however, that the industry is
totally guided by consumer demand. If there is a demand
for more expensive, additive free food, the consumer shall
have it. If the consumer wants dull uninteresting food, that

is much less convenient to use, it will be provided. If they want bread that goes mouldy in two days instead of five, here it is. If information is of prime importance, here are the labels and the pamphlets and the books and the videos and all the paraphernalia of good communication. We shall be better informed and probably none the wiser.

This seems, under the guise of consumer sovereignty, an ill-concealed declaration of war on nutritional education and standards. Wright seems more interested in the origin of consumer hostility to additives. She cites food activists as a significant factor whom she remarkably characterises as overpowering the food industry:

> These organisations and individuals have considerable media skills – a talent acknowledged by food industry personnel and one which they feel unable to match and so, often refuse media opportunities themselves . . . for fear of being 'out manipulated' by these adversaries.
>
> (p. 82)

This is hardly credible given the resources available to the food industry,[43] and a more likely explanation for such media shyness is the weakness of their case rather than their inability to put it. Significantly, the substance of the issues becomes displaced by a bizarre stance on relative media skills, just as the tag 'extreme' is applied to food activists to cloud the substance of what they have to say.

The net result is the attempt to marginalise food activists and structurally separate them from legitimate and legitimised influence. One index of this is the lumping together of food activists with the sensationalism of the press. The strength with which such strategies of marginalisation must be pursued follows on from the complexity and, to some extent, the fragility of the food information system itself, in so far as it has been opened to waves of fashion that might at times incorporate the influence of 'extremists'. For those involved in the food information system, the issue is posed of whether they are to be complicit with the imperatives of the food system or to combat it more effectively.

Just as commerce does not confine itself to profit-making, nor is government solely neutral or, more exactly, benevolent in its own dissemination of food information. It responds to economic and political interests which can dominate the trickle-down of CHNT even if this were an appropriate model for it to put to work. It may be captured by food industry interests or even be concerned over adverse publicity and its own survival. Consider, for example, Mayhew's (1988, p. 457) account of the results of a nutritional survey of 1931 which

> found only half the country was living at a level of nutrition so high that on average no improvement could be effected by improved consumption, and also – because of the effect of large families on family budgets – a fifth of the country's children were chronically undernourished.

A later survey with a sample of 5,000 very closely confirmed these findings. Yet government, rather than acting upon these results, successfully served to suppress them. Why was this so?

> At a time of mass unemployment, low wage labour and fiscal retrenchment, government ministers and civil servants were desperately concerned to disprove links between malnutrition, ill-health and low income.

It is against such historical precedents that we should judge government's commitment to the health of the nation's diet, an issue taken up in the final chapter.

5

AGRICULTURAL SUPPORT AND DIET

Introduction

This chapter focuses on the relationship between agricultural policy and diet. It does so by addressing two very different cases. In the first section, an assessment is made of the literature dealing with the impact of the European Union's Common Agricultural Policy (CAP) upon the consumption of food. Surprisingly, despite acknowledging the cost of the CAP and the extent to which it distorts agricultural prices, this literature draws the conclusion that there is very little impact on the level and even the composition of food consumption. However, it is argued here that this conclusion rests upon a counterfactual analysis which is dubious in method and limited in scope, setting aside the way in which the CAP is an integral part of the food system and how alternative policies with a genuine commitment to healthy eating could have a larger and potentially beneficial impact.

This conclusion depends in part upon the case study of Norway in the second section, although reservations are also raised about the ease with which policies for healthy eating can prevail over commercial food interests. Norway has been held up as an example to emulate because of its apparent success in integrating food and health policies. However, this integration has always favoured agricultural interests in practice. Initially, it proved possible because expanding dairy production was perceived to be in conformity with the country's dietary needs. Once this proved to be false, as coronary heart disease became associated with excessive fat consumption, policy continued to favour the dairy sector despite its apparent inconsistency with dietary guidelines. The famed Norwegian integration of food and health policy has been reduced to informational campaigning, with dairy production continuing to benefit from economic support.

In each of the two case studies, we have not undertaken analysis in detail, especially in putting forward alternatives. Rather, our purpose is more to question the way in which the issues concerned have been addressed. For the impact of the CAP on diet, there is a need to cast the analytical scope much wider than the role played in shifting supply curves. This is well illustrated by the Norwegian outcome, where the attempt to shift demand through health policy has been circumscribed by the continuing power of the dairy industry.

CAP and the nation's diet

Popular antipathy towards the EU's CAP has become considerably attenuated in recent years, especially as the focus of media attention has shifted to the impact of 1992 (the creation of a single market) and the cases for and against the European Monetary System (EMS) and a single EU currency. In addition, concerted attempts to address the problems of surplus production have drawn criticism away from the most overt symbol of the CAP's negative impact, the creation of unsold food in the form of 'mountains' and 'lakes'.[1] Nevertheless, evidence would appear to suggest that the impact of the CAP has been and continues to be significant. As Table 5.1 indicates, CAP expenditure has continued to increase over recent years and still commands over half of the EU's budget, even though its share has declined as other EU programmes have been introduced and expanded.[2]

Table 5.2 indicates the levels and distribution of costs and benefits from European Community policy in 1986/7 relative to those of the USA (which employs a wide range of agricultural support policies)[3] and Japan (which seeks self-sufficiency in rice). For the UK,

Table 5.1 Expenditure and the EU budget (billion ECU)

	1989	1990	1991	1992	1993	1994
Total budget	40.9	44.4	53.8	61.1	63.5	73.3
CAP budget	24.6	26.3	31.9	33.6	35.9	37.2
CAP share (%)	60.1	59.2	59.2	54.9	56.5	50.8

Source: Ockenden and Franklin (1995, p. 21).

Table 5.2 Costs of agricultural support, 1986/7 (billion ECU)

	Producer benefit	Consumer cost	Taxpayer cost	Net cost	Transfer ratio*
USA	26.3	6.0	30.0	9.2	1.4
EC	33.3	32.6	15.6	14.9	1.5
Japan	22.6	27.7	5.7	8.6	1.5

Source: Colman and Roberts (1994).

Note: * ratio of second plus third to first column

the cost is estimated at that time to have been around £16 per week for a family of four. As Gardner (1996, p. 81) puts it:

> New Zealand farmers get 5 cents (US) a litre for their milk; EU farmers get 30. This is why the NZ dairy industry can ship butter 13,000 miles round the world to Europe and still undercut British farmers by 25 per cent in their own market – or they would do if Brussels didn't slap a 25 per-cent tax on the imports to stop them from benefiting UK consumers in this way.

Table 5.3 shows one estimate of the effect that the CAP has had on EU prices, raising them for sugar by only 6.3 per cent but by as much as 57.5 per cent for butter. The CAP has also had substantial effects on world market prices as the EU's surplus production is exported at considerably lower prices than are realised within the EU and with a depressing effect on world market prices (at the expense of export revenue for other food producers). Between 1980 and 1986, for example, the EU's volume of exports increased by 36 per cent, whilst those of the USA declined by 33 per cent and those of other developed countries only increased by 19 per cent. Estimates of the negative impact on world prices range to as high as 30 per cent for dairy products.[4] In addition, CAP surplus exports contribute to the volatility of world prices, responsible for over 50 per cent of price fluctuations for wheat and dairy products.[5]

Whilst this paints a picture of the CAP as providing continuous support to agriculture, the latter has been changing significantly with rapid increases in productivity and farm size and substantial reduction in numbers of farms and employment. The share of agriculture in EU GDP had fallen below 3 per cent by 1991, with only Greece (16.1 per cent) and Ireland (8.1 per cent) above 5 per cent.

Table 5.3 Consumption effects of the CAP

	Average price* 1988–92	Price* effect of CAP	Price change (%)	Effect on demand (%)	Weekly consumption† per person 1992	Estimated weekly consumption† per person w/o CAP 1992
Milk	29.3	6.9	23.5	-0.29	-8.1	1.69	1.83
Cheese	156.7	51.6	32.9	-1.20	-61.5	4.01	6.48
Beef	195.8	67.6	34.6	-1.25	-69.8	4.98	8.46
Pork	147.8	12.1	8.2	-1.73	-15.9	2.53	2.93
Poultry	105.4	8.8	8.4	-0.13	-1.1	8.18	8.27
Eggs	103.7	11.6	11.2	n/a	n/a	2.08	n/a
Butter	106.9	61.5	57.5	-0.55	-60.2	1.44	2.31
Sugar	29.1	1.8	6.3	-0.24	-1.5	5.51	5.60
Bread	27.1	1.9	7.1	-0.09	-0.7	26.62	26.79
Rice	58.3	5.5	9.4	n/a	n/a	1.33	n/a

Source: Cawley *et al.* (1994) using OECD estimates of prices and MAFF estimates of elasticities.

Notes: * pence per pound † ounces, except for milk (pints) and eggs (dozens)

Employment share stood at 5.8 per cent with over 30 per cent of farmers also holding a second job.[6] These changes need to be set against the original objectives of the CAP as laid out in Article 39 of the Treaty of Rome, 1957:

1 The common agricultural policy shall have as its objectives:
   (a) to increase agricultural productivity by developing tech-nical progress and by ensuring the rational development of agricultural production and the optimum utilisation of the factors of production, particularly, labour;
   (b) to ensure thereby a fair standard of living for the agricul-tural population, particularly by increasing the individual earnings of persons engaged in agriculture;
   (c) to stabilise markets;
   (d) to guarantee regular supplies; and
   (e) to ensure reasonable prices in supplies to consumers.
2 In working out the common agricultural policy and the special methods which it may involve, due account should be taken of:

(a) the particular character of agricultural activities, arising from the social structure of agriculture and from structural and natural disparities between the various agricultural regions;
(b) the need to make the appropriate adjustments gradually; and
(c) the fact that in Member States agriculture constitutes a sector which is closely linked with the economy as a whole.

It is generally acknowledged that in practice the second of these objectives, 1(b), has been the driving force behind policy, although reservations are expressed over whether this is an appropriate target and appropriately targeted. For Swinbank and Tanner (1996, p. 34), for example:

It is no exaggeration to claim the farm income objective has dominated CAP policy making from the outset. This is despite the fact that it is far from clear what is meant by a 'fair' standard of living, who is to be included in the 'agricultural community', and what levels of farm income are actually attained, or that item (1b) above is really linked to item (1a) . . . which implies that increased incomes are dependent upon increased productivity.

They go on to observe that the different policy objectives may conflict with one another and no ranking nor weights are attached to them. In addition, the nature of the objectives as well as the policies to pursue them will differ according to the diversity of farming conditions and product-type. Most significant in terms of the stated goals of the CAP is the meticulous critique offered by Hill (1996). He simply observes that in order to formulate, let alone implement, policies for support to the level and stability of farmers on low income, it is necessary to have systematic data on sources of income by farming *and* other activities by different types of farmer. Otherwise, it will be at best a matter of supporting farming and not low farmers' income, thereby including those who already have high incomes from farming and/or other sources. As he concludes from his research:

In the light of these findings it seems incontrovertible that, in assessing whether the 'fair standard of living of the agricultural population' mentioned in the Treaty of Rome is being approached, it is necessary to include all forms of income flowing to that population. Low incomes cannot be assessed on one part of income alone, especially as the income from farming seems to be a particularly unreliable guide to total income on small farms where income problems could be anticipated. And the comparability of the incomes of farmers with those of other groups in society cannot be judged in the almost total absence of reliable statistics.

(p. 210)

Nor is this, then, an academic point, as a high proportion of farmers do derive a significant proportion of their income from other sources. Indeed, they are positively encouraged to do so under the guise of reducing agricultural supply of goods and increasing efficiency. In such circumstances of poor identification of policy targets and poor methods of targeting, it is hardly surprising that the major beneficiaries of the CAP should be large-scale producers on high incomes, even if their smaller counterparts also shelter for a time under the umbrella of support prior to being eliminated.

It is against the background of the longer term changes in EU agriculture that reform of the CAP has been introduced from the mid-1980s. The literature has witnessed a corresponding and distinct shift in emphasis. From primarily criticising the costs and inefficiencies of the CAP at the economic level and interrogating how these conditions could be tolerated at the political level, the literature has now moved towards forecasting the impact of the CAP reforms, in conjunction with incorporation of the interaction with and effects of the Uruguay Round, whilst explaining how such reforms could have been politically feasible. Despite these changes in emphasis, the methods both for economic and for political analysis have remained unaltered. For the economics, as discussed in more detail below, it is a matter of shifts along or shifts of supply curves as the agricultural support system is reformed. For the politics, the (not so) new political economy approach is adopted. The power of the farming lobby is generally perceived to have declined with its falling numbers of employees and farms and its weight within economic activity.[7] In addition, reform has been driven by external pressures arising out of the Uruguay Round of GATT (now the World Trade Organisation) which eventually incorporated measures for agriculture. Difficulty lay primarily in coming to a settlement between the USA and the EU, including its constituent members.[8] Whilst EU output has been restricted in a number of ways, beginning with milk quotas in 1984 and leading to the MacSharry reforms in 1992 which made provision for set-aside, the marriage of GATT and MacSharry has not reduced the levels of CAP expenditure in the short run as producers are compensated for not producing (set-aside) and, in the longer term, outcomes are liable to be subject to continuing (re)negotiation.[9]

This cursory overview of the CAP is intended to indicate the extent to which it is both embroiled in a complex set of arrangements around agriculture and is a significant part of those arrangements. A more complete account would need to go into detail by incorporating a broader range of influences as well as including the differences across both countries and crops as well as the complexity and variety of the CAP policies themselves.

In particular, much of the literature is marked by the following failures. First, it does not explain the CAP policies sufficiently since what has been perceived to be the traditional goal of supporting low income on farms has been notably absent except as a side-show and rationale within political ideology. This is despite the media hype that always surrounds the highly visible blockades that accompany farmers' direct action in response to shifts in the CAP policies. These give a false impression of the political clout of small farmers. Rather than representing the tip of the political economy mountain, they are at most its distant foothills.

Second, there is considerable neglect of the other agents involved in the CAP food systems, not least those further along the food chain but before the impact is felt by consumers. Traders, processors and retailers have a considerable interest in how food is produced and at what prices. Nor are they without political influence.[10] Global wholesaling and retailing, for example, can themselves bring about shifts in economic interests depending upon whether what are often the few firms concerned choose to support a strategy of protection of their own domestic markets or access to the markets of others.

Finally, as is even indicated by the varying impact of the CAP by product, how these various factors fit together is differentiated from one commodity to another. Simple economics and simple politics do not suffice to deal with the specificities of beef, sugar, dairy, and so on. This is a matter not of a corrective by provision of more details but of identifying the specific structures and dynamics of the individual food systems.

In short, the literature on the impact of the CAP tends to neglect systemic analysis even though it does itself recognise it in unsystematic fashion from time to time. Swinbank and Tanner (1996, p. 13) refer favourably to the notion of 'world agriculture in disarray', the title of the book by Johnson (1973) which has been influential in understanding agricultural developments since the 1970s. The notion is associated with falling commodity prices and farm incomes, growing commodity stocks and tax burdens, and increased tension in international trade negotiations. To these, Gardner (1996, p. 100) adds growing farm size and productivity, biotechnology, environmental considerations, and the differentiation of crops between those serving bulk and niche markets. Is this all reducible to shifting supply and demand curves?

Nonetheless, despite the shortcomings characteristic of the conventional framework with its narrow if generalised approach, enough of the literature has been covered to suggest on its own terms that the CAP has had a considerable impact. For Swinbank (1993, p. 371), summarising his review of the latest round of reforms: 'Consumers (and the food industry), taxpayers, and overseas competitors with some justification claim that the CAP remains a very distortive and costly policy.' Paradoxically, however, exactly the *opposite* conclusion has been reached by the literature when the issue is addressed of the influence of the CAP on what we *eat* rather than how much we pay. As Cawley et al. (1994, p. 10) conclude: 'It seems likely that the CAP will have had relatively little effect on total food consumption in the UK or on its broad composition.' Moreover, this view does not revise a prevailing conventional wisdom to the contrary, for Cawley et al. survey seven other papers on the issue[11] and conclude that they are all consistent with their own findings:

> This section surveys the contributions made by these authors to the study of the effects of the CAP upon nutrition and assesses the extent of any consensus amongst them. As might be expected, there are several common ideas running through these analyses. Perhaps slightly more surprising, for a group of economists, is the measure of agreement amongst the authors.
>
> (p. 13)

As is recognised by Cawley et al., such analyses are generally based upon counterfactual hypotheses. The effect of the CAP is assessed by comparing actual, empirically known, outcomes in which it is present with the hypothesised or counterfactual situation in which it is absent. Clearly, the conclusions depend entirely upon the specification of the counterfactual. Although extremely popular, as in what would have happened if Germany had won the Second World War, counterfactual analysis raises serious problems. One such problem, as is acknowledged by Cawley *et al.*, concerns indirect effects. The simplest way to assess the counterfactual is to assess direct effects alone. If I take away these two bananas from this bowl, then there will be two less fruit in it. On the other hand, this might induce further indirect knock-on, potentially compensating effects. I will eat less of the remaining fruit or even replace those that have been hypothesised to have been removed – even with an even larger number in a bunch! I might even take all the fruit from the bowl on the grounds that it looks better either full or empty but not somewhere in-between. One conclusion, then, is that counterfactual analysis can make very simple events seem very much more complicated.

Cawley *et al.* use the indirect effects in their counterfactual to argue that direct effects alone will exaggerate the impact of the CAP. They give three reasons for this within their analytical framework, which is to assess the effect of the CAP on prices and the effect of prices on consumption through food demand. First, if we gauge the impact of the CAP by the extent to which it increases individual prices, this will overlook the potential to substitute between foods from the higher to the lower priced. Also the impact of the CAP cannot be measured by the difference between EU and world prices, since the latter would be considerably higher in the absence of the depressing effect on prices of the CAP-induced exports. The impact of the CAP across different foods is liable to be greater than the impact upon food as a whole. Second, even so, farm prices are only a proportion of food retail prices, at most one-third on average, with processing, retailing and other costs having accounted for an increasing proportion of food prices over time. Consequently, the impact of the CAP on farm prices is diluted in its effect on food prices and, hence, upon consumption. Third, Cawley *et al.* reasonably argue that the removal of the CAP would leave a gaping policy vacuum – it is not as if agriculture was previously without support – which would almost inevitably be filled by an alternative. This would have to be taken into account and would, presumably, involve some degree of cost and have some effects, if not necessarily as significant as those of the CAP itself.[12]

It is important to recognise that the third indirect effect is of a different analytical status than the other two. For they are the direct and indirect *consequences* of the CAP and are presumed to occur or not in association with it. On the other hand, the need to replace the CAP with alternative policies is an implicit recognition that the CAP is an *effect* of other causes even if it does itself have further effects. Thus, the CAP is both cause and effect amongst the determinants of food consumption.

Once this possibility is recognised within counterfactual analysis, it raises a much more serious problem than that of direct and indirect effects – that is, the question of its status and meaning altogether. If the removal of the CAP simply has the effect of inducing an alternative, even equivalent, set of policies, does this mean that the CAP has no or limited effect? A simple example will be illustrative even if at the expense of bordering on the facetious. Does an umbrella stop us from getting wet when it rains? The role of an umbrella in this respect is readily understood, like the fruit example earlier. What light would counterfactual analysis shed on the matter? If the umbrella is taken away, we would get wet. Yet, if this induces a replacement umbrella, the full effect would be nil, as would the rather different option of staying indoors. Now this example could be pursued further to explore the motives for going out and the costs and availability of replacement umbrellas. However, the point is rather to demonstrate that counterfactual analysis is necessarily partial in its scope.

This is most apparent in the standard analysis of the impact of the CAP which is found to be replicated in text after text.[13] This assumes the existence of a given demand curve for agricultural products. Through price support, the CAP is presumed to shift the supply curve to such an extent that demand is exceeded, creating a surplus that must be stored or exported at lower and lowered world prices. Moreover, as productivity increases over time, the cost of the CAP increases and creates pressure for budget reform, which is resisted by farming interests and their political representatives.

Even if the calculation of the impact of the CAP is not as crude as this in Cawley *et al.*, it does contain the same essential features. As can be seen from Table 5.3 on p. 99, the impact upon selected items of consumption are small with the exception of cheese, beef, pork and butter. The figures are calculated from the effect of the CAP in conjunction with the estimated price elasticities of the foods concerned. In short, accepting the estimation of price effects, the impact of the CAP is simply reduced to the price effects on demand as derived from given consumer preferences. On this basis, the conclusion is almost inevitable and, in a sense, has nothing whatsoever to do with the CAP! For, as it is implicit within this analysis that prices are only a minor factor in the determination of the level and, to a lesser extent, the composition of food expenditure, it is hardly surprising that the CAP should have been limited in impact if considered for its influence through the price mechanism alone.[14]

If, however, the CAP has not been influential in determining food consumption, what has played that role? For Swinbank (1994) and Ritson (1991), the answer lies in factors that are independent of the CAP. Swinbank (1994, p. 201) concludes:

> What is certain, however, is that the CAP, despite its massive impact on raw material supplies, does not have a dominant role in determining the food we eat: our international buying power, and the ready availability of foods on world markets, are more potent considerations.

Thus, trends in the provision of food and income are central although they remain unexamined, and it is not established that they have no causal or systemic relationship to the CAP itself, even though the latter is associated with social stability in rural areas and has served to guarantee markets in response to rapid increases in productivity. Similarly, Cawley *et al.* identify dramatic changes in the trends in the demand for foods, but, once again, these are taken to be independent of influence through or from the CAP. This is clear in the anticipated impact of the removal of the CAP on beef and butter. Do we really believe that at least half as much again of each of these would have been consumed in the absence of the CAP despite the extent to which consumption has declined over recent years? Cawley *et al.*'s procedure is to net out the major trends in consumption and then to calculate the (CAP) price effect. But if the price effect had been that big, it would almost certainly have modified the trend itself.[15] In short, the counterfactual method essentially asks the following question: leaving aside the major determinants of supply and demand, what would have been the effect on consumption of removing the CAP? The answer is hardly surprising as it is guaranteed by the nature of the question.

Is there an alternative to such counterfactual analysis? As previously remarked, the method is itself limited, even counterproductive. An alternative approach to the CAP would contain the following elements over and above those traditionally included. First, note that the counterfactual treatment of the CAP is *not* food-specific. The shifting supply and demand curves and even the more sophisticated calculation of elasticities could, in principle, be applied to any product. Where the uniqueness of food is recognised, it is only through its special features in terms of supply and demand – that the weather and fertility are uncertain, that land supply is constrained, that there is a tail of low-income producers, and so on. As has been argued here and in Fine *et al.* (1996), food is different from other products in view of its organic properties and how these are incorporated into its specific systems of provision as a whole.

Second, then, it is insufficient to focus upon agriculture alone (and an agriculture in which the role of landed property is effectively unexamined despite reference to surplus and differential productivity). How has it been incorporated into the chain of activities that make up the food systems? In addition, it is totally inappropriate to separate out the dynamics of the food system as trends around which the CAP is a price- and quantity-adjusting mechanism. The CAP is an effect of the tensions that arise out of the process of agricultural development. It cannot simply be wished away as a counterfactual.

Third, it follows that it is necessary to address the shifting role played by the food industry. Its absence, other than as an unseen conduit between agriculture and consumption, is notable in the counterfactual approach and peculiar, given the new political economy approach to agricultural policy. Why have not food industry interests prevailed over those of farming? To some extent, this can be explained paradoxically by the high level of concentration within the food industry and the capacity to exploit oligopolistic markets within the individual countries of the EU. With the single market of 1992 and increasing diversification across the food industry, whether by manufacturers, wholesalers or retailers, it is hardly surprising that interest in price supports for agricultural products should weaken. This is liable to be intensified when the EU food industry seeks further diversification into markets outside the EU, especially if various barriers to trade are reduced.

Fourth, it is important to disaggregate the impact of the CAP both by country and by product. The factors previously outlined have a different weight and are integrated in different ways, each potentially with a different dynamic and structure. For this reason, in Fine *et al.* (1996) we examined the UK sugar, dairy and meat systems separately rather than in conjunction with their counter-parts in the EU as a whole.[16]

Finally, it is crucial to recognise how the food systems function to generate the demand for their products, although they do not have sovereign control over this. From our perspective, elaborated in Fine *et al.* (1996), it is nonsensical to consider that the consumption of sugar and butter, for example, would have been reduced by the CAP by virtue of its impact upon prices. On the contrary, their consumption has been sustained through the support to their production and the use of that additional supply within the food systems, even if at higher prices and with some export of surplus.

It follows that the counterfactual analysis is inadvertently an appropriate reflection of the motivation underlying the CAP – its preoccupation with agricultural supply with no account taken of the demand for food and, by implication, the health of consumers. As Cawley *et al.* (1994, p. 16) report from previous studies:

> Any beneficial nutritional impacts that have occurred as a result of the CAP are purely accidental: there are no explicit health or nutrition objectives within the CAP and such an outcome has certainly never represented a delib-erate intention of the Council of Ministers.

Were the counterfactual to take up an alternative to the CAP in which agricultural, food and health policy were integrated, then its current impact would be perceived to be considerable and damaging. However, it is precisely because the CAP is oriented around farming that it precludes health considerations. Significantly, where the role of the EU on healthy eating is addressed, it tends to be done separately from agricultural policy, even if with equally depressing prospects within these limits, as standards are under pressure to be reduced to the common minimum. In the following section, it is shown how the coordination of agricultural and health policy can have significant effects in altering the form that each takes; but that a significant and positive outcome depends upon health considerations prevailing over commercial food interests.

Lessons from the Norwegian experience: the exception that proves the rule

Nutrition policy has now become an established part of the respon-sibilities of the governments of developed countries. But, as

Kjaernes (1994a) has observed, nutritional policy differs substantially in form, extent and content, whether from one country to another or with the passage of time. This is hardly surprising since the origins and factors behind the formation and implementation of nutritional policy are multi-faceted and complex in how they interact.

First, nutritional policy has a historical dimension in which it responds to shifting conditions, as with growing affluence. Initially, at lower levels of development, policy has been primarily concerned with adequate levels of food consumption and a safe and hygienic supply of food. This provided nutritional policy with a focus upon adequate supplies of food at sufficiently low prices and the targeting of households vulnerable to inadequate consumption in view of low income and/or inappropriate spending patterns. As will be readily recognised, such concerns over the hard to feed have not disappeared but they have been complemented or even displaced by preoccupations with the diseases of affluence.[17] Nutritional policy has been concerned with *reducing* overall levels of consumption as well as modifying the composition of diet.

Second, the evolution of nutritional policy depends upon developments within nutritional science and its perceived relevance to the health of the nation. Thus, the origins of nutritional policy, beyond the provision of enough to eat, are to be found in the identification of essential nutrients, such as vitamins, which might be absent from a typical diet. Again, such concerns have been turned upside-down in the current era with the discovery that chronic diseases can in part be a consequence of overconsumption of standard ingredients in the modern diet, such as fats and salt. The advance of nutritional science in these respects is contested both within the research community and from those whose commercial interests are liable to be damaged by the practical application of the results of research. The evolution and impact of nutritional science is, then, both cause and effect in the evolution of nutritional policy. The latter depends upon the progress and acceptance of nutritional science and an acknowledgement of its significance for a sufficiently broad section of the population.[18]

Third, nutritional policy necessarily represents the resolution of conflicts of interest, however unsatisfactorily or impermanently. In particular, those commercially engaged in the provision of food will be affected by nutritional policy, and this has to be set against a more nebulous construction and representation of consumer interests. Because policy responds to commercial interests in a variety of economic arenas (trade, science and technology, taxation, and so on), issues crucial to nutritional policy are liable to be decided upon independently of the health concerns around food, which tend to be placed in a separate ghetto and limited to an exclusive focal point within health policy. Further, the balance of economic interests, as well as the strengths and directions with which they are pursued, shift over time and with economic development. Thus, it is generally recognised how important have been farming interests in determining agricultural policy but, equally, that privileged state support can vary with the relative weight of agriculture within the economy.[19] However, whilst agricultural policy is liable to have a profound impact on nutritional outcomes through the supply of food, nutritional policy has tended to have only a limited purchase over this or other policies that lie outside its immediate compass. More generally, then, nutritional policy falls institutionally between a number of stools straddling agriculture, industry, commerce, health and welfare, science and the environment, and so on. Thus, quite apart from the variety of sources seeking to influence nutritional policy, there is liable to be fragmentation in its formulation and implementation. This has been recognised in analyses of nutritional policy by appeal to theories of the state supplemented by network theory, in which diverse interests and agencies are perceived to have a shifting influence over policy through shifting institutional mechanisms.[20]

Fourth, nutritional policy has been influenced by a variety of factors that are not always directly or predominantly food-related. Effective concern with food poverty, for example, has more readily prospered in a Keynesian-welfare context where a more favourable political and ideological stance generally prevails towards the responsibilities of the state for the well-being of its citizens. Even so, the role of the state in this respect has always represented a balancing act between individual and social responsibility, with a difference in balance from one country to another according to its traditions. In addition, the diseases of affluence have arisen at a time when, at least ideologically, the boundaries of welfarism have been on the retreat. In the case of nutritional policy, this has reinforced the notion of individual responsibility, since the latter is genuinely seen as more readily feasible. Whereas there might always have been some residual doubt and moral scruples over the ideology of self-help in face of poverty and food scarcity, this seems less plausible when individuals apparently have the option of a healthy diet. Moreover, apart from nutritional policy being influenced by more general political and ideological factors, it is also subject to the particular cultural content of food itself. Healthy eating, for example, can be associated with green politics, with national customs and with the preservation of rural traditions – hence encompassing, and potentially combining, a wide spread along the political spectrum between extreme radicalism and extreme conservatism.[21]

Finally, the evolution of nutritional policy is dependent upon its impact and how this is reacted to and incorporated. If dietary guidelines are set but not met, what happens? The answer will reflect two different but closely related aspects. On the one hand, it depends upon the extent to which the determinants of nutritional outcomes are correctly identified and genuinely addressed by policy with commitment to succeed. Inevitably, this requires a broadening of the scope of policy and a strengthening of its incidence and coherence. This is because, on the other hand, nutritional policy will – in an apt terminology – induce feedback effects which may moderate, nullify or even overwhelm the intended effects. For example, informational campaigns on healthy eating are liable to be uneven in their impact. Those consumers who are more responsive to such campaigns are liable already to have healthier diets. Their reduced consumption of potentially unhealthy foods can lead to a shift of this consumption to those who already have the inferior diets. Alternatively, the introduction of healthier products, such as skimmed milks, will entail the reincorporation of the milk fat in other products, such as cream and cheeses, again possibly to the detriment of those already with the worst diets. And the creation of an ethos of a healthy diet can be appropriated by the food industry to expand the range of food products made available, even thereby encouraging overconsumption by virtue of that variety alone, as well as because of the false ideology that consumption of a supposedly healthy food exonerates the consumption, in addition, of a supposedly unhealthy food.[22]

Against this general background discussion of the evolution of nutritional policy, consider the specific case of Norway. It is of particular interest because it is often held up as being uniquely successful. A recent report by the Scottish Office (1993), highlighting the extreme dietary deficiencies in Scotland, goes much further in its recommendations than other earlier UK nutritional policy documents, with their emphasis on health and informational campaigns. It recognises the need for and seeks substantial change all the way along the food system, although considerable weight still rests on information, education and personal food choice. The 'integrated Norwegian model' is picked out for special praise, specifically for 'bringing many organisations, including the commercial sector, together to develop policies for improving the nation's diet' (p. 83). In particular, the farming industry had been incorporated.[23] Consequently: 'By involving the agriculture and food industries in a responsible approach to progressive dietary change, Norway was able to avoid much of the conflicting advertising, lobbying, sponsorship and diversionary questioning of the scientific evidence seen in other countries' (p. 84).

What stands out then is that the form in which Norwegian nutritional policy has been adopted is one which institutionally incorporates agricultural, and other, interests with the effect of coordinating and smoothing policy implementation. This does not, however, in and of itself guarantee that the content of nutritional policy is satisfactory. For it depends upon the nature of those farming and other commercial food interests and the extent to which they are influential in policy formulation and implementation. Clearly, from the perspective adopted here, nutritional policy needs to take account of the impact and feedback effects of agriculture as well as the rest of the food system. This is certainly neither more nor less important by virtue of formal integration of farming interests.

The relevance of these remarks is borne out by the recent and growing critical literature on the Norwegian experience. First of all is highlighted the dependence of the current integral model on its historical origins in the 1930s – the age of food scarcity and prior to the diseases of affluence when nutritional policy and agricultural policy could be readily developed in harmony with one another. In particular, the heavy dependence of Norwegian agriculture upon dairy production dovetailed with the image, informed by the then nutritional science, of milk and butter as healthy foods worthy of increased supply into the foreseeable future. In many ways, the only blot on the horizon concerned the commercial threat posed by margarine, which could be industrially manufactured from non-dairy sources of fat. Significantly, this was resolved by legislating for a required butter content in the manufacture of margarine. In part, this also signified the strength of agriculture relative to the fishing industry, which had the potential to provide whale oil as a margarine ingredient.

In short, Norwegian nutritional policy has been integral more in terms of agricultural interests incorporating health policy than vice versa. This is also a way of interpreting the advantages that are often perceived to have been influential in promoting an integrated nutritional policy. These include the small population (four million), lack of ethnic minorities and a strong nationalism and national culture, a commitment to preservation of a rural way of life and, in the more recent period, the space for leeway in economic policy created by the oil wealth bonanza.

Clearly, however, in the post-war period, comfortable cohabitation between agricultural and health policy could not persist. Coronary heart disease in Norway became particularly severe and was associated, not without initial contestation, with high levels of dairy product consumption. By 1975, a new National Food and Nutrition Policy had been formulated (Milio, 1990), but it remained within the same previously established policy structure despite the immanent conflict between health and agricultural interests (Kjaernes, 1993a). Responsibility fell upon the National Nutritional Council (NNC) to formulate and campaign for policy. Whilst a political and institutional space had been created for its activities, its room for manoeuvre was severely constrained. With the interests of nine ministries to coordinate (Jensen *et al.*, 1986), it only had two staff members before 1979 (Milio, 1990)!

The NNC's limited influence initially is illustrated by the fate of low-fat milk. It was not until 1984 that it was introduced in Norway (compared to 1969 in Sweden and 1973 in Denmark) (Brandtzaeg and Kjaernes, 1987; Kjaernes, 1993b, 1994b; Kjaernes and Jensen, 1994). Although skimmed milk had previously been made available, it had not proved acceptable to consumers. Low-fat milk became acceptable to agricultural interests once policies were in place to ensure the availability of markets for the otherwise discarded cream.[24] As Jensen (1994, p. 103) documents, agricultural prices were set to guarantee the consumption of total production: 'Institutions faced with applying the nutrition policy accept the necessity of selling the total agricultural output.' Just as in the interwar period, butter was to be mixed with margarine. Cream was to find commercial outlets in desserts, yoghurt and cheese. Jensen *et al.* (1986, p. 8) observe: 'The resulting paradox can be summed up as follows: *Eat less fat, but more butter.* It also seems true that the *nutrition policy will have all individuals to eat healthily, as long as they together consume all agricultural products.*'

Consequently, the apparent uniqueness of Norwegian nutritional policy in integrating and coordinating the different aspects involved in policy formulation owes much more to its historical origins than to points of departure in resolving conflicts with, and prevailing over, commercial (agricultural) interests. Norway is unusual in its degree of dependence upon dairy. This, together with other special features, allowed nutritional policy to be formulated in novel ways. But its uniqueness in content should not be exaggerated. In the era of food shortages, expansion of supply can be harmonious with nutritional policy (subject to competition with margarine!). Putting such policies into place, let alone into reverse, in deference to shifting dietary guidelines is much more problematical, especially where there is a much wider variety of foods and interests to accommodate. Thus, the very same factors that were favourable to the creation of an integral policy in Norway in the earlier period have continued to prevail, but so apparently have the economic interests of dairy farming, which are no longer perceived as compatible with a healthy diet. This contrasts with the process, if not entirely with the outcome, in the United States, for example, for which Nestle (1993) identifies dozens of lobbying groups on behalf of the food industry which had the capacity to delay and modify healthy eating advice in the form and content of the 'Food Pyramid'.[25]

Yet, in Norway, even in these historically more favourable circumstances, with well-defined objectives and relatively few and transparent opposing commercial interests, successful intervention has been limited and circumscribed. Jensen *et al.* (1986, p. 9) suggest that 'it is not very far from truth to say that the nutrition policy to some degree has acted like a tool in the hands of agricultural interests' and, even more sharply, 'summing up, from our point of view the Norwegian nutritional policy is unhealthy' (p. 21). Nutrition policy has continued to be driven by the need to avoid conflict with the farm-food industry (Jensen *et al.*, 1986; Milio, 1990). As Hill (1992) has observed in the same context for UK and US nutritional policy, conflicts of interests are resolved, or avoided, by focusing exclusively on informational and educational campaigns. For Jensen *et al.* (1986, p. 12):[26]

> But, from our point of view it is important to understand *why the informational campaigns are chosen: When actors with diverging and partly opposing interests are put under pressure to do something they will be tempted to use informational campaigns.* Informational activities involve neither obligations nor problems with legislation and organization. Such activities will also give high political visibility in a short time. It is rather easy for strong actors with conflicting interests to

disobey information and to counteract the effects with marketing and low-price campaigns.

In conclusion, even in what is presumed to be the ideal case of Norway, the form taken by nutritional policy in order to compromise with opposing interests is primarily through reliance upon informational campaigns. Whilst these have some impact, even apart from the counterweight of the advertising and informational campaigning of the food industries, they are themselves subject to feedback effects which can be counterproductive. If a lesson is to be learnt from the Norwegian experience, it is one that suggests a strategy not of emulation but of greater commitment and scope of intervention to ensure desired outcomes in transforming the nation's diet. Policy must go beyond exhortation and accommodation of commercial interests.

6

WHITHER FOOD POLICY?

The mid-nineties will, in retrospect, stand out as remarkable for the dramatic change that occurred in UK food policy. At the time of writing (April 1998), the newly elected Labour government had, within a year of coming into office, issued a White Paper (MAFF, 1998), recommending that a new Food Standards Agency (FSA) be established. The thinking and policies incorporated within the White Paper represent significant breaks with the past in a number of respects. First, and foremost, an independent agency will be created with the powers both to commission and to publish research and to make recommendations for the formulation of policy.

Second, however, it is important to recognise what is meant by 'independence'. In part, it is relative to government as a whole. The FSA will be able to act within its powers without, for example, requiring any prior ministerial approval. However, one of the key elements in the emergence of an independent FSA is the scarcely veiled dissatisfaction with the regulation of food standards that has evolved under the Ministry of Agriculture, Fisheries and Food (MAFF) and, to a lesser extent, other ministries with food-related responsibilities such as the Department of Health. Of over-whelming significance in this context is the idea that MAFF in particular has, in principle, been faced with a conflict of interest in which it has simultaneously sought to marry the commercial inter-ests of agriculture and the food industries with those of the public as food consumers.

In practice, however, reference to independence in the context of the need for a separate FSA signifies an assessment not so much that MAFF has been caught between conflicting interests as that it has too readily come down on the side of commercial as opposed to public interests. Even if MAFF's traditional reputation for being the ministry responsible for sponsoring agriculture has been tempered in recent years, it has only been because of a more favourable attitude to the food industry as a customer of agriculture. The ultimate consumer has been last in line as far as MAFF is concerned. Now such priorities are to be reordered with the independent role to be played by the FSA, which is also intended to address the fragmentation and unevenness of policy making and enforcement, with current divisions of responsibility lying across MAFF and the Department of Health and between central and local government. The FSA will take over some of the responsibilities previously falling under MAFF.

In short, the FSA is intended to be independent against a background of previous lack of independence in food policy and, in particular, through MAFF, the predominance of commercial over public interests. Consequently, independence of the newly formed FSA must also be guaranteed through the composition of its membership and through its practices of calling upon equally independent sources of advice, an implicit acknowledgement of the extent to which food research and advisory committees have been unduly influenced by commercial interests.

Such changes in the institutions through which food policy is to be made are matched by an equally significant shift in thinking. For, third, it is explicitly accepted that the FSA will need to review the provision of food along the entire food chain. This opens the possibility for independence in so far as all activities and interests are incorporated from hand to mouth, and not only those wedded to commerce.

Fourth, whilst it is the representation of the public as consumer that is seen as being promoted by the greater independence attached to the newly formed FSA, a parallel but distinct shift in representation is also involved. Specifically, over the past decade or more, many grass-roots groups of food activists have emerged and campaigned vigorously, if only with limited success.[1] Now these groups are taken much more seriously and, rather than being scurrilously labelled, treated and dismissed as food terrorists, their activities and opinions are being incorporated into the conventional wisdom, and leading individuals are even becoming part of the food establishment.

There is, then, no doubt that major change is afoot. Its prospective impact, however, has to be assessed with considerable caution, not least because current proposals are primarily institutional and not substantive in content. Further, the ethos of establishing independence that informs the presentation of the proposals is equally limited in substance. For the latter resides in the conflicts of interest within the food system. These need to be identified and policy stances adopted relative to them. This task has been allocated to the FSA, and the independence with which it is supposed to carry out its duties is to be welcomed. But there is a presumption that conflicts of interest are resolved by such independence rather than changing the balance of circumstances in which they are fought out. The James Report (1997), which was commissioned for the Labour Party whilst in opposition and on which the White Paper is based, suggests:

> What is needed, is a new body which separates the role of protecting public health and safety from that of promoting business. An Agency must operate openly so that decision-making becomes more transparent and the true balance of interests is subject to public scrutiny.
>
> (p. 14)

Who could disagree? Notably, the principles involved have little to do with food as such. Nor is there a general case for a separate agency to accommodate conflicts of interest or principles – commerce versus health and safety. It depends upon the powers, practices and ethos that govern such agencies both in their internal workings and their external environment. For example, in the interwar British coal industry, the conflict between safety and productivity in the mines was resolved by handing responsibility for both to the single 'agency' of pit deputies. The result was to sacrifice safety to commerce (Fine and Harris, 1985, Chapter 11). Similarly, there is no guarantee that the independent FSA will not be subject to 'regulatory capture' unless the principles of conflict resolution are laid down, set in the wider context of how the food system functions, and health and safety is ensured as the first priority.

That such considerations are germane follows from the overt motivation for, and impulse behind, the White Paper. Whilst it does itself make little reference to them, the James Report is explicit about the 'force for change'.[2] It has derived from the food scares of the previous decade, beginning with (the persisting) salmonella in eggs and chickens,[3] and peaking with the 'mad cow' drama, which still continues at the time of writing. Quite apart from how well these food scares have been handled, both the James Report and the White Paper take as their most important consequence the undermining of public confidence in the provision of food and the public agencies responsible for food health and safety. It is almost as if change is necessary for change's sake in order to restore confidence to a disillusioned public. The White Paper, for example, tediously refers to risk and public confidence a dozen times or so in its opening pages. For the James Report:

> Social science research reveals a widespread distrust of government, science and business and of any regulatory authority seen to be close to vested interests . . . public information and education in themselves are an inadequate means of coping with the public's crisis of confidence. The public need to have faith in the systems that are intended to protect them and confidence in the decision-making process in these complex issues.
>
> (p. 15)

It follows that the stimulus to reform derives from the response to food scares, and the proposed reforms are heavily marked by such origins. As previously observed in Chapter 4, however, the food concerns that most hit the headlines are not necessarily the ones which warrant the most attention from a health perspective. In particular, even if the food scares serve as a striking and, in part, appropriate metaphor for the prevalence and consequences of commercial interests, they are totally misleading in addressing the three concerns covered in this book – eating disorders, the compatibility of agricultural with food policy, and the sources and use of nutritional knowledge.

Not surprisingly, then, the proposed role of the FSA in nutritional and dietary matters is at most token. Further, although the James Report has incorporated, mainly implicitly, the lessons to be learnt from experience of other countries,[4] there is no place for international comparisons in the White Paper. Is it established that the proposed food regulation has functioned more satisfactorily elsewhere and, if so, to what extent, and with what lessons for the UK? In any case, the critical review offered of the Norwegian experience in Chapter 5 here, establishing the difficulty of coordinating food and agricultural policy, is notable for its absence in providing lessons for the UK.

Instead, what we are offered, apart from the new agency itself, is the determination that consumers should have the ability to make 'informed choices'. Keane (1997, p. 179) acutely observes that whilst the Health Education Authority was allocated £700,000 to spend on nutritional education in 1996/97, over £550 million was spent on advertising food and drink in 1995. In such circumstances, as well as for other reasons, as has been argued in Chapter 4, notions of informed choice are a recipe for confusion in the context of food. Much informing and much choice takes place through the functioning of the food and food information systems that exist alongside, interact with and undermine the intent of the trickle-down of healthy eating knowledge from a supposedly independent FSA, even if it inspired public confidence. Indeed, the launch of the White Paper was accompanied by reassurances that the government had no intention of acting as food police or authoritarians. People would not be told what to eat, at least by government – although it was to ban the sale of beef on the bone within a few weeks to a chorus of accusations of interference in individual liberty. As Keane (1997, p. 179) concludes:

> Healthy eating is clearly a political issue and the majority of 'information' about food and health is driven by commercial considerations, particularly in terms of advertising and product descriptions and, more implicitly, by the government's reluctance to intervene in the 'freedom' of the market. This reluctance to intervene is in contrast to highly interventionist policies pursued in relation to food production, particularly since the introduction of the Common Agricultural Policy.

In conclusion, the proposed FSA is to be welcomed if only with one cheer or two. It does potentially remove the institutionalised advantage of commercial interests in the formation of food policy. It promises a degree of openness. But each of these should already have been the starting point for making policy in any area. What remains disturbing is the emphasis on food safety, the lack of adequate consideration of coordination of agricultural and food (and health) policy, and the continuing belief in informed choice. Equally puzzling, given the lack of attention to nutrition, diet and health, is the extent to which the proposals have been welcomed by food activists as if much of their work has now been completed. On the contrary, it has only just embarked upon a new beginning.

NOTES

1 INTRODUCTION AND OVERVIEW

The first section of this chapter is, in part, based upon a talk delivered to the Institute of Historical Research, University of London. Thanks to comments from participants, especially Anne Murcott.

1 For an assessment of the world food problem from the perspective of malnutrition, see Dyson (1996). Fine (1997a) provides a critical survey of the entitlement debate deriving from Sen (1981).
2 Delahoyde and Despenich (1994), for example, estimate that US cattle consume five times the grain of their human counterparts.
3 See also Fine *et al.* (1998).
4 For an overview of the programme as a whole, see Murcott (1998).
5 Interestingly, if by coincidence, at least in her title, Varney (1996) also refers to strawberries. Her study is concerned to unravel the relationship between food, toys and gender. Implicit is the need to address particular foods; less recognised is the role played by individual food systems as a whole.
6 For an alternative view of the heterogeneity of money in terms of the uses to which it is put (which could then apply even more so to food), see Zelizer (1994). For a critique, see Fine and Lapavitsas (1998).
7 See also Glennie and Thrift (1992, 1993) and Fine (1993).
8 The approach derives from Merton (1957). For a critique, see Mills (1959) and, in the context of segmented labour market theory, Fine (1998a).

2 RESOLVING THE DIET PARADOX

This chapter is based on Fine (1993).

1 The categories covered are culinary cultures, food ethnology, nutritional trends, food and health, eating disorders, patterns of food consumption, shortage and plenty, food technology, the impact of colonialism and migration, professional cookery and eating out of the

home, domestic cookery, division of labour in the home, and food in institutions.

2 This is the distorted form of Brillat-Savarin's original claim, 'Tell me what you eat and I will tell you what you are.'

3 'Tell me what you read . . .' is perceived to be an important component in identity and functions as a device for the definition of the consumer through targeted advertising. Indeed, earlier empirical work on the patterns of ownership of consumer durables proved possible through use of the National Readership Survey, which functions as a service to advertisers by collecting data on household characteristics, including reading habits, together with consumption patterns.

4 It has, for example, been much more usual to use other indicators of social class. For a discussion of food and class, see Fine *et al.* (1996, Chapter 11).

5 Similarly Alberto-Fidanza (1990) sees food as increasingly assuming the characteristics of a language – as a mode of agreement, protest, revenge, power, and so on, at both an individual and group level, again drawing the parallel with clothing.

6 See Chapter 1 for a brief discussion and Fine *et al.* (1996, Chapters 3 and 4) for an extensive argument.

7 This then leads to a literature concerning the impact of nutritional deficiency on bodily function, not only in relation to morbidity and mortality but also for work capacity, and so on. See Waterlow (1990) and Spurr (1990), for example, and also Popkin and Lim-Ybanez (1982).

8 See Pelto (1987), for example.

9 See also Harris *et al.* (1984) and Doan and Bisharat (1990).

10 See, however, the account of the tension between human nutrition (as a science) and the social sciences in Kornberg (1976).

11 Lupton (1996, p. 155) questions whether we know less and less about food as we become more distant consumers.

12 Mennell (1987) discusses shifting patterns of food consumption in terms of the civilising appetite. Turner (1982) provides a link through Foucault to power and the physical control of the body.

13 See, for example, Bogin (1991), Manderson (1987), Pelto and Pelto (1985) and Kornberg (1976).

14 On food faddism, see Stare (1976), Belasco (1989), Kandel and Pelto (1980) and Apte and Katona-Apte (1980).

15 See also Pill and Stott (1982) and Davison *et al.* (1991) for an account of popular epidemiology.

16 See Charles and Kerr (1988) for the emotional stress arising out of the comfort and anxiety associated with food.

17 See Chapter 3.

18 Or that the income elasticity of demand is less than one; in general, it is usually posited that the income elasticity declines with income.

19 See Houthakker's entries in Eatwell *et al.* (eds) (1987). For reviews of demand theory in economics, see Brown and Deaton (1972), Deaton and Muellbauer (1980) and Blundell (1988).

20 For a critical assessment of such empirical studies in practice in the context of the UK National Food Survey, see Fine *et al.* (1996, Chapter 7).

21 Note that Naik and Moore (1996), working on food expenditure as a whole, find that there are significant habit effects on consumption (lags in changing how much you spend), but that these vary in extent across individuals.

22 Why economists should set themselves the task of maximum explanation on the basis of given preferences, a common theme within the work of Becker even across generations, must appear as bizarre, to non-economists, as it is unjustified.

23 See Fine (1997b and 1998b) for a critique of Becker.

24 See Gardner (1992) for a review of the literature on the 'farm problem'.

25 Unless expenditure shares are independent of prices, as for the Cobb–Douglas utility function, for example.

26 As in Lancaster's notion of the characteristics of goods, with the added twist of allowing these characteristics to serve as the raw materials for household production.

27 Anderson (1988) finds for Hong Kong that the proportion of income spent on food increases with income as hospitality is expanded.

3 THE POLITICAL ECONOMY OF EATING DISORDERS

This chapter is much revised from Fine (1995a), extending the scope from anorexia to consider other eating disorders and taking into account subsequent literature.

1 On food scares, see Miller and Reilly (1994).

2 The BMI is defined as mass in kilograms divided by the square of height in metres. What is considered to be a healthy level is itself a social construct which is recognised to vary over time and individuals. It varies, for example, from 21.4 for those in their twenties to 26.6 for those in their sixties. (See West, 1994.)

3 It is necessary to be acutely aware that much of the discussion of the issues covered in this chapter – in analysis, diagnosis and treatment – attaches pejorative connotations to deviation from what is presumed to be normal. All the concepts employed are socially constructed in the fullest sense but cannot be avoided easily, giving rise to unintended judgements with moral overtones. As will be seen, varying stigmas are attached to the different eating disorders. These have to be identified and explained rather than taken for granted. Thus, anorexia, for example, can reasonably be viewed as an ordered and understandable response to a specific social and personal environment rather than as a simple deviancy.

4 They conclude:

Almost half of the White women and one quarter of the Black women who are trying to lose weight at any particular time are not overweight by the usual definition. Although most report using generally accepted weight loss practices, 13% – close to 2 million women in the United States – are using clearly unhealthy strategies such as fasting; vomiting after eating; and taking diet pills, diuretics, and laxatives. The average normal-weight female dieter reports a lifetime weight fluctuation that is 50% greater than that of her nondieting counterpart. Hence, she may be incurring increased risk of coronary disease and premature death as a consequence.

(p. 716)

5 Colditz (1992) suggests that 34 million US adults were obese in 1980. He attributes the economic costs of obesity in 1986 as follows, taking account of indirect costs of morbidity and mortality discounted at 4 per cent non-insulin-dependent diabetes $11.3 billion; cardiovascular disease $22.2 billion; gall bladder disease $2.4 billion; hypertension $1.5 billion; breast and colon cancer $1.9 billion. If account were taken of muscoskeletal disorders, a further third would be added to the overall figure.

6 Robison *et al.* (1993) estimate dieting services at $30–$50 billion.

7 He also points to an £80 million industry for meal replacement slimming products and £5.5 million expenditure on slimming magazines in the mid-1980s.

8 See French and Jeffery (1994), who observe that the measurement of dieting is problematic and that dieting may have other adverse effects even if correcting the diseases of being overweight. Kirschenbaum and Fitzgibbon (1995) also question whether dieting as a cure may be worse than the disease, but, taken together, the contributions advise moderation and the prospect for improvement in efficacy in the future through more experience and research. A further problem is that the impact of dieting is itself highly variable depending upon body-weight, genetics, metabolism, lifestyle, age, and so on. (See Brownell and Rodin, 1994.)

9 Stein (1991) places bulimia at an incidence of between 1 to 3 per cent of various samples of young women. He points to the extent to which it has been exaggerated in the popular media.

10 See Brumberg (1992, p. 149), for whom 'familiarity with eating disorders may well be implicated in their increase'.

11 For an account of the early diagnosis and treatment of anorexia, see O'Connor (1995). Her emphasis is, however, on the medical interpretation of the condition, not its causes as such.

12 For a critique of the various theories of consumption across the social sciences, see Fine and Leopold (1993, Part II).

13 See Fine *et al.* (1996, Chapter 7).

14 See also Scarano and Kalodner-Martin (1994) and Bordo (1993, pp. 49, 60) for the notion of eating disorders as representing a continuum rather than a break with normal eating behaviour more generally.

15 With a corresponding health and media industry associated with diagnostic drift, fashions in diagnosis, copy-cat incidence, support

organisations (such as Anorexia Anonymous) and popular fiction (see Brumberg, 1988). Butler (1988) reports 59 medical and scientific papers in 1973 and 165 in 1982. The *International Journal of Eating Disorders* was set up in 1982 to address the issues associated with anorexia, bulimia and obesity (see Gordon, 1990). It acknowledged Princess Diana on the cover of the issue following her death – did any other academic journals do so? Rothblum (1990) finds that the first reference to weight and dieting occurs in *Psychological Abstracts* in 1955. For an overview of the literature on eating disorders, see Brownell and Fairburn (eds) (1995).

16 Of course, these disciplines are used to trying to discover why some smoke and others do not, and how much, but they are much less frequently used in treatment of the consequences in the form of cures.

17 The discussion that follows draws heavily upon the literature but with only selective referencing – the themes that are highlighted recur again and again, as the reader can confirm even by a casual review of the thousands of contributions available.

18 Note that Bordo (1990) sees androgyny as symbolising liberation from gendering, but also as a yuppie sign (Bordo, 1993). Turner (1987) takes obesity as signifying women having escaped a degree from the control of men.

19 See Bordo (1993, pp. 245ff.) and Brownell and Wadden (1992). Thompson (1993) reports that, by 1988, over two million Americans, 87 per cent female, had undergone cosmetic surgery, a tripling over the previous two years. There is a death rate from this surgery of one in 30,000.

20 See Sanftner *et al.* (1995) for a discussion of the distinction between shame (attached to long-term dissatisfaction with self-image) and guilt (concern over short-term specific acts) and their relationship to eating disorders. Andrews (1997) suggests a chain of causation from childhood abuse to shame, and from shame to bulimia.

21 See Rolland *et al.* (1997), Thompson *et al.* (1997) and Sands *et al.* (1997) for recent studies of pre-adolescent concern for body image and diet.

22 Although the obese can compensate for such prejudice by greater self-regard (Miller *et al.*, 1995).

23 Crandall (1995) finds that parents discriminate against obese daughters in not providing them with finance for a college education. Ironically, female freshers serve as the most favoured target for case studies of eating habits and disorders, suggesting that discriminating parents may inadvertently be doing their daughters a good turn by not exposing them to the extreme pressures to be thin! Johnson and Wilson (1995) report on the legal status of weight-based discrimination. Cooper (1997) considers the ethics of the fat woman designating herself as disabled.

24 This raises the issue of the direction of causation between obesity and mental disorder, since the latter may arise out of the stigma attached to the former rather than being its source. See Allison and Heshka (1993) and Mills (1995) apart from the work of Rothblum.

25 Sjostrom (1993) accepts that there has been inadequate rigour in the research investigating the ill-effects of obesity, accepts that more sophisticated measures are necessary, but argues this does not lead to the view that there are no ill-effects. See also West (1994).

26 Joiner *et al.* (1995) emphasise the inter-relationship between body dissatisfaction, bulimia and depression.

27 For Wolf (1991, p. 163): 'The anorexic body is sexually safer to inhabit than the pornographic.' She also cites a figure of 150,000 deaths per year from anorexia in the United States.

28 Consequently, feminism has been blamed as a factor in the creation of eating disorders, especially anorexia, because of the tension it creates between accepting and rejecting traditional female roles. For a rebuttal, see Bordo (1993) and Bailey and Hamilton (1992).

29 Frederick and Grow (1996) suggest a link between lack of autonomy, self-esteem and eating disorders.

30 See Polusny and Follette (1995), Calam and Slade (1994), Moyer (1997) and Dansky *et al.* (1997). Andrews *et al.* (1995) find past child-hood abuse more liable to lead to depression in mothers, and eating disorders, especially bulimia, in their daughters. Weiner and Thompson (1997) find that even covert sexual abuse is associated with eating disorders.

31 Pike (1995) posits that bulimia may result less from life dissatisfaction *per se* and more from the absence of a network of family and friends that allows for conflict to be aired and resolved. Van den Broucke *et al.* (1995) find an association between eating disorders and lack of marital intimacy. Esler (1995), however, suggests that the search for common patterns of family behaviour, constellation or style has proved unsuc-cessful, and that the notion of an elusive 'anoregenic family' is an obstacle to successful research.

32 Suzuki *et al.* (1995) find that both school males and females are more subject to bulimia if engaging in alcohol abuse, but this is also the case for smoking for females.

33 For the strata of young women concerned, it is almost inevitable, for example, that educational performance and the teenage transition will coincide. The same applies to other symptoms, rendering impossible an assessment of the exact importance of each.

34 Bleau (1996) argues that high levels of dietary restraint and anxiety are conducive to eating disorders. In the case of ballet dancers, being closer to ideal weight is more likely to lead to aberrant eating patterns (Kaufman *et al.*, 1996).

35 See Macdiarmid and Hetherington (1995) for a study of chocoholics who exhibit greater cravings and less self-control, and set short-term satisfaction against long-term guilt.

36 Schafer *et al.* (1994) observe that when marriage breaks down, the impact on dietary 'self-efficacy' is much more disturbing for women than for men, emphasising the importance of food to women's daily lives and self-esteem in general. Whitehead (1994) points to the importance of the relationship between domestic food provision and domestic violence.

37 Davis and Yager (1992, p. 377) report that 'throughout the last decade the prevalence and clinical features of eating disorders have been delineated in middle to upper class Caucasian females from Westernised countries in a large number of studies from the United States, Canada, and Western Europe'. More recent research, however, has suggested that socioeconomic status has been exaggerated as a factor in eating disorders (Rogers *et al.*, 1997). Card and Freeman (1996) suggest diagnosis and treatment have been the source of a self-fulfilling myth in establishing bulimia as a disease of higher status young women.

38 See Emmons (1992), who finds that black girls are more likely to use diuretics and laxatives whereas white girls rely more upon vomiting. See also Powell and Kahn (1995), Striegelmoore *et al.* (1995), Parker *et al.* (1995) and Greenberg and LaPorte (1996) for a variety of perspectives on the differences in eating disorders by race. Note that Szmukler and Patton (1995) recognise that eating disorders are cross-cultural but that they are associated with westernisation. As Bordo (1993) argues, it is always important not to accept the racial stereotypes that often accompany explanations for the differing incidence of eating disorders, particularly that black women have different body images which means that they tend to be fat, whereas white women tend to be anorexic.

39 See also Murnen and Smolak (1997), who find that eating disorders are more associated across the sexes with the attributes of femininity rather than masculinity.

40 Of course, such correlations can be informal. As Bryant-Waugh and Lask (1995, p. 13) observe, 'much of the literature is anecdotal and lacking in critical content'. My favourite example is the consultant psychotherapist who confesses to having experienced a flash of inspiration in recognising that anorexia is associated with familial preoccupation with appearance, even if neither a necessary nor sufficient condition, (Lieberman 1995). Speed (1995) perceptively adds that men primarily examine and women suffer eating disorders.

41 See also Spurrell *et al.* (1997) for the significance of whether first eating disorder is as binge or diet.

42 There can also be eating disorders by proxy, with mothers displacing their symptoms to their daughters, as suggested in Scourfield (1995), even to a 2-year old (Honjo, 1996).

43 This is correctly recognised by Lupton (1996, p. 133) in terms of the control and not the loss of appetite. Note that she sees this as a specific form of a more general condition of modernity: 'In consumer culture there is, therefore, a continual dialectic between the pleasures of consumption and the ethic of asceticism as means of constructing the self: each would have no meaning without the other' (p. 153).

44 See Rosen *et al.* (1986).

45 Mennell (1987, p. 374), therefore, inappropriately employs the analogy of appetite as a thermostat that might be too high (bulimia) or too low (anorexia). Appetite is, rather, potentially more complex, in being more than one-dimensional as in temperature, and contradictory.

46 See Smuts (1992, p. 526) who observes that 'Many women in modern industrial societies appear to be caught in a punishing conflict between powerful evolved mechanisms designed to make them fat and powerful modern motivations to be slender.' However, he pursues this in a bizarre Darwinian framework of natural selection. Smith (1993) also correctly places considerable emphasis on the simultaneous pressures both to eat and to starve but attaches these primarily to media messages, with the presumption that the lower (upper) classes are more amenable to eat (diet) propaganda, thereby explaining the relative incidence of eating disorders. See also Turner (1987, p. 104): 'Anorexia in part expresses a certain social contradiction between mass consumption and the norm of thinness through the practices of restraint and dietary management.'

47 As Beumont (1995, p. 157) observes: 'About a third or more of patients considered for treatment at eating disorder clinics do not fulfill the diagnostic criteria of either anorexia or bulimia nervosa and are classified as atypical.'

48 See Martz et al. (1995) for emphasis on connections between female gender role stress (FGRS), body image and eating disorders. More generally, see Szmukler et al. (eds) (1995) for contributions searching for appropriate environmental, physiological, genetic, motivational and sociocultural factors.

49 See a sequence of articles on this in the *International Journal of Eating Disorders*, in which a particular measure is often taken of ideal bodily shape, itself serving as an index of the pressure to diet, namely the ratio of bust to waist size in media representation of women.

50 More generally:

> In the clinical literature . . . attempts to link eating disorders to one or another specific pathogenic situation (biological, psychological, familial) proliferate, along with studies purporting to demonstrate that eating disorders are members of some established category of disorder (depressive, affective, perceptual, hypothalamic . . .). Anorexia and bulimia are appearing in increasingly diverse populations of women, reducing the likelihood of describing a distinctive profile for each. Yet the search for common pathologies still fuels much research. As each proposed model is undermined by the actual diversity of the phenomena, ever more effort is put into precise classification of distinctive subtypes, and new 'multidimensional' categories emerge . . . that satisfy fantasies of precision and unification of phenomena that have become less and less amenable to scientific clarity and distinctness. . . . Where a unifying element *does* clearly exist – in the cultural context, and especially in the ideology and imagery that mediate the construction of gender – the etiological significance is described as merely contributory, facilitating, or a 'modulating factor'.
>
> (p. 49)

NOTES

In this vein, the intention in this chapter is, of course, to place economic as well as cultural factors in their rightful position.

51 MacSween provides an excellent, critical assessment of the literature on anorexia from a fully developed sociological perspective. See also Bordo (1993).

52 Its clinical history dates back to the diagnosis by Richard Morton in 1694 (Butler, 1988). See also Stein and Laakso (1988) and Casper (1983).

53 Equally, this raises the issue of whether contemporary eating disorders are the same irrespective of the symptoms and characteristics of the individual, as for pre-adolescents compared to young women (Wren and Lask, 1993).

54 For a counterexample, see Banks (1997), who finds current cases of religiously inspired eating disorders with no apparent concern for bodily image.

55 See also Brumberg (1988, pp. 46–7), van Deth and Vandereycken (1995), Ziolko (1996), Silverman (1995), Parry-Jones and Parry-Jones (1995), Brownell (1995) and the reviews of Lee (1995, 1996), who attaches eating disorders to culturally specific contexts, especially modernisation rather than westernisation. Lowe (1995) identifies the transition to eating disorders in wealthy female students in 1920s US colleges.

56 Although this is beginning to change as the topic spreads across the social sciences, just as does the incidence of eating disorders themselves.

57 See, for example, McNay (ed.) (1992) and Meehan (ed.) (1995).

58 See Fine et al. (1996, Chapter 10), where recent trends in meat consumption suggest that gratification through some forms of food has become more important to the worse-off, reversing previous patterns of consumption.

59 See Brumberg (1988, pp. 259–60) for a cursory examination of some other factors drawn from political economy, such as market fragmentation.

60 A particularly disturbing aspect of this conflict is the extent to which young women take up unhealthy smoking in order to have a 'healthy' (i.e. reduced) appetite.

61 These are discussed in Fine et al. (1996) in terms of the 'organic' properties of food.

62 Brownell and Wadden (1992) report the presence of 35 million food vending machines in the United States.

63 The superstore, in particular, provides a bewildering array of products and product varieties, intensifying the pressures to purchase, and the range of displaced emotional contents associated with food. As Bowyer (1988, p. 169) observes:

It is because of the vast choice of foods available that anorexics are so unsure of what to choose and on what basis to make choice. Decision-making over food becomes a painful task and going to a supermarket can be a paralysing prospect because of the extensive choice available.

64 See Fine and Leopold (1993, Chapter 6) for a critique of the concept.

65 An earlier slogan in the UK for ice cream to be purchased from mobile vendors.

66 The 'Death' brand of cigarettes, which positively advertises itself as causing cancer, proves an exception, especially as it seeks publicity by offering a share of its profits in support of cancer research. This, in turn, creates moral dilemmas for the anti-smoking lobby in so far as it has to choose whether to take the money and promote cancer and cancer research simultaneously. The parallel with the pressures to eat and not to eat is clear but exceptional. Tobacco advertising prefers to promote a healthy image in its advertising directly or through the support of healthy activity, such as sport. An example of smoking and not smoking at the same time is in cigarette-like products that allow for nicotine-free sucking and holding.

67 The literature is extensive, but see Waller and Shaw (1994). Andersen and Didomenico (1992) find that magazine ads are ten times more likely to promote dieting in women than in men. A large number of studies also seek to investigate whether children watching TV, especially in the United States with its high level of advertising of foods for children and child viewing, is correlated with eating disorders, specifically obesity – through the mechanisms of their eating more and exercising less. The results are far from establishing a strong effect, even though Robinson *et al.* (1993) report 6- to 11-year olds watching 23 hours and 12- to 17-year olds 21 hours per week. However, this tends to overlook both the simultaneous media representation of thinness, to which young girls are extremely sensitive, and the potential for TV ads to establish and have an influence on patterns and levels of eating and exercise that become common both to those who watch TV and those who do not through a transmission mechanism based on the former.

68 See Henderson and Vickers (1995), who also observe how women are confused between dieting for health and for beauty.

69 In this context, experimental evidence is created by investigating responses to images of self and others that have been distorted by video.

70 This is brought out especially strongly, but implicitly, in Falk's (1991) discussion, following Rozin (1982, 1990), of how one form of representation of food can be developed into its opposite – from bad to good to eat, for example. Unfortunately, this seems to be seen as chronologically sequential rather than simultaneously contradictory. Nor are these potential tensions linked to the ways in which foods are provided rather than received, as is discussed below. More generally, it is remarkable how little anthropologists have contributed to the understanding of anorexia, given their analytical potential to explore the tensions between the different roles and meanings of food.

71 MacSween (1993, p. 211) seems to draw a narrower canvas:

Eating as morality versus eating as indulgence is a central opposition in anorexia ... [and] is separated into two strictly
separate categories. 'Safe' food, which is nutritionally valued,
low calorie, and not 'fattening', is sanctioned as either doing the
body good ('health' foods) or at least not causing any harm
('diet' foods). 'Dangerous' food, food which is off the list, is
dangerous because it is food as pure pleasure, which does all
harm and no good.

72 The strength of counter-culture within capitalism, even where
commercialised, should not be underestimated. The same applies to
the pillaging of the past for the purposes of marketing. See, for
example, Bordo's (1993) discussion of the shifting shape of Madonna,
with her early stand for a fuller figure with resonances with Marilyn
Monroe, generally recognised to signify the last fashion watershed in
the drive to thinness, but her ultimate subordination to present-day
norms. It would take too many Madonnas, with too much non-
commercial commitment, to undermine the dynamics and structures
that tie the food and body image industries together.

4 DIGESTING THE FOOD AND INFORMATION SYSTEMS

This chapter draws heavily upon Fine and Wright (1991).

1 See Walker and Cannon (1985) and Robbins (1983, p. 1351):

The industries' effectiveness in lobbying against [dietary] goals
should not be underestimated ... The industries prefer vague
statements which cannot be interpreted to show the degree of
change necessary by industry or consumers.

2 For an exception, see Sanderson and Winkler (1983, p. 1354):

To be effective, therefore, nutrition policy must move beyond
educating individual consumer-patients toward a balanced
strategy involving all interested parties ... changes in the
national diet will have economic, social, and political consequences all along the chain.

A strategy is identified as needing education, substitution (of good for
bad foods), pricing, provision (in government institutions) and
regulation.
3 See Wright (1990) and Wright and Howcroft (1992) for a sketch of
sources of food information.
4 The other stages she employs along the way are scientific reviews, text-
books and consensus reports, popular books, magazines and
newspapers, and advertisements and health claims.

5 For the latter stage, see Burkitt (1994), who argues that the absence of western diseases, such as certain cancers, in developing countries provided the clue for identifying the importance of fibre in the diet and the dangers attached to over-processing of food. See also Milio (1990).

6 Ashwell (1992) points to publication bias in scientific research in that papers with statistically significant results are more liable to be submitted and published than those that are not, and studies funded by industry take precedence over those funded by government. Scientific reviews of literature show bias in citing studies that support the author's view.

7 For a particular example of the role of government in influencing the reporting of results, see Miller and Reilly (1994) and Reilly and Miller (1997) on food scares.

8 See Scott and Worsley (1994), Caswell and Padberg (1992) and Guthrie et al. (1995).

9 See Bennett et al. (1994) and Viswanath et al. (1993).

10 See Frewer et al. (1994) and Caswell and Padberg (1992).

11 Sheiham (1991) finds that most people's understanding of healthy eating is broadly in line with the nutritionists, but gaps in knowledge and misunderstandings have led to confusion. See also Sheiham et al. (1990).

12 See Strychar et al. (1993) and Rodgers et al. (1994), for example.

13 See Levy et al. (1993), Auld et al. (1994), Beggs et al. (1993), Reid and Hendricks (1993) and Cremer and Kessler (1992). Murphy et al. (1995) find that children know much about healthy food but do not act upon it. Are adults so much different? Kelder et al. (1995) find that multiple interventions are necessary to sustain the health message and its translation into a healthy diet; Holm (1993) shows how hard it is to sustain a healthy diet even once it has been adopted.

14 See also Domel et al. (1993), who find that exposure to fruit and especially vegetables is important for inducing a preference for them.

15 Robbins (1983), Sanderson and Winkler (1983) and Walker (1983) emphasise the need for consumers to switch between products and for producers to change their products' composition. See also Scottish Office (1993).

16 Cole-Hamilton et al. (1986) claim to demonstrate that NACNE guidelines were not draconian, in the demands placed upon the consumer, by monitoring the success of a sample of dietitians and their households in consciously modifying behaviour. Their study essentially reveals the difficulties experienced even by those best placed to succeed, especially in keeping up energy levels whilst reducing fats, sugar and sodium. See also Gibney (1990), who links such problems to the inconsistency of dietary guidelines – reducing fat through drinking less milk may lead to anaemia, for example.

17 See also Bradby (1997), who examines the food beliefs of young Glaswegian women of Punjabi descent and finds them to derive from two different sources corresponding to 'their' and 'our' food, and from medical and traditional advice, respectively.

18 Even though this is well known not to be so. For an early review, see Thomas (1979), for whom:

> Having looked at several aspects of the relationship between knowledge and eating behaviour it seems clear that food practices do not change just because people are in possession of accurate factual knowledge. On the other hand, we may find that those making the wisest food choice, are in fact, people with the highest levels of knowledge.
>
> (p. 164)

19 See also Black and Rayner (1992), whose assessment of the relative merits of different forms of labelling indicates the limited impact of them all, with consumers making greater use of background nutritional knowledge than of information on packaging.

20 Schapira *et al.* (1990) point to the difficulties of consumers in translating their knowledge into practice. Shepherd and Stockley (1986) find that consumers' attitudes towards fat consumption are more important than nutritional knowledge.

21 See also Whichelow (1988), who finds that commercially advertised products with fibre content are best identified as such compared to generic commodities.

22 See also Roberts (1991) and MAFF (1987).

23 However, the medical profession is usually noted for its lack of knowledge of healthy eating (see Schapira *et al.*, 1990, for example).

24 For McKie and Wood (1991), the quantity and quality of information provided is a source of confusion. Working-class women in north-east England 'are likely to retain a level of cynicism tempered by budgetary constraints and the dietary preferences of household members as they continue to purchase and prepare food' (p. 28).

25 This is not necessarily so for developing countries where advertising in the context of healthy food finds high levels of credibility (see Musaiger, 1985).

26 Campbell and O'Connor do, however, recommend 'a generic set of guidelines for overall policy based on ample reliable evidence and generous scientific consensus' (p. 91).

27 See the dispute between Wilkins (1994) and Casson (1994) in the context of branded products, with one welcoming the information that is incorporated in such products in terms of guarantee of quality, and the other, respectively, perceiving consumers as being duped.

28 Lefebvre *et al.* deny that they are concerned with 'social control' but seek 'a method of empowering people to be totally involved and responsible for their well-being' (p. 148).

29 See Tobin *et al.* (1992) for a discussion of the issues involved in the collaboration between professionals and the food industry. They conclude:

> The formation of such alliances may be sensible and fruitful for some purposes, but when the goal to be addressed is public

education, it is essential that the public's health and nutritional well-being be the primary consideration for *both* parties.

(p. 306)

The emphasis is added to question whether this condition can be met given the imperatives of profitability that govern the food industry.

30 See also Kirk and Arens (1988), for whom 'A unique opportunity exists for harnessing commercial motivation and communication expertise for the benefits of consumer nutrition education' (p. 268).

31 For an extended critique, see Fine and Wright (1991) and Fine and Leopold (1993).

32 Some of their work has been brought together in Ippolito and Mathios (1989, 1996). Note their contributions take place against what is judged to be a continuing assault on the US Food and Drug Administration (FDA) from the far right for its having undermined freedom of action and choice, even though there is something of a cosy relation with big business (Nixon, 1996). For a review of US food policy, observing the emphasis on the consumer (choice) rather than the producer (supply), see Lane (1995).

33 See also Ippolito and Mathios (1994a, p. 202):

> For example, if a producer focuses on the low cholesterol content of its product and is gaining market share from the claims, a competing producer that has a low cholesterol *and* low saturated fat product has the incentive to spread this informa- tion to regain the lost sales. This competitive process should provide a fuller picture of the range of products available in the market than is provided by individual claims in isolation.

34 Caswell and Padberg (1992) report that one third of food advertising in the USA incorporates a health claim. It amounts to a cost of $5.6 million per day for the largest advertisers and as much as $2 million per day for the twelfth smallest of food sellers.

35 See Lien (1995) for an elaboration of the contradictory roles and goals portrayed in food advertising.

36 See Kotz and Story (1994) and Taras and Gage (1995). The first study finds, for a sample of over five hundred food ads (56.4 per cent of all ads directed at children), that the most frequently advertised products were high-sugar cereals and that 43.6 per cent of ads covered foods categorised as in the fats, oils and sweet category. The later study, comparing data following the introduction of new regulations, found that cereals and sweet snacks were advertised to a lesser extent, but were displaced by other foods (processed, canned and prepared foods) equally high in fat, salt and sugar. See also Delahoyde and Despenich (1994), which shows how the fear of vegetarianism has led the US meat industry to advertise meat to children by deploying connections to the latest toys and fads in vogue. Consumers International (1996) survey the international experience of television advertising targeted at children, finding that food accounts for the highest proportion by far

and, in the UK for example, 95 per cent of advertisements were for products high in fat, sugar and/or salt.
37 See Ippolito and Mathios (1994a, pp. 200, 216).
38 For the UK, see Fine *et al.* (1996, Chapter 11).
39 They do, however, find that their results are uneven across different foods and nutrients and across different socioeconomic strata.
40 Where theory is used, it tends to be drawn from psychology. See also Glanz and Rudd (1993), for whom, in a study of nutrition education and consumer behaviour professionals:

> The theories that were most familiar to the respondents were also considered to be the most 'current' in both fields: social marketing, consumer information processing, and social learning theory.

Most revealing is the finding that:

> A paradox became evident: when asked their general opinions about the value of theory for guiding research and of research for guiding the practice of consumer nutrition education, respondents were usually neutral or pessimistic. This suggests that those surveyed were skeptical about the operationalization of theories for research and practice, and about the conduct of applied research with clear implication for practice. They considered the concepts in this survey to be important, but not readily available or consistently used for research and practice.
> (p. 272)

41 For a discussion of food and the left, see Lang (1986/7).
42 See Keane's (1997) study of responses to healthy eating advice, which reveals a healthy scepticism 'in the context of an information system that they perceived to be based on the needs of the producer rather than the consumer' (p. 190).
43 As Sanderson and Winkler (1983, p. 1353) note: 'But with a budget of only £8.5 million, the Health Education Council cannot counteract the advertising of the food industry, which spends £400 million a year to increase consumption, not reduce it.' Similar relative budgets presumably exist for public relations.

5 AGRICULTURAL SUPPORT AND DIET

1 Other popular accounts of the impact of the CAP include reference to the more or less legal gaining of subsidies through movement of commodities across national boundaries. Thus, Gardner (1996, p. 30) reports wheat from France being loaded off a ship at one end for the briefest of landings at Hamburg before being loaded on again at the other end in order to benefit from a $17 per tonne subsidy to wheat of *German* origin. As Gardner observes, the support accrued to traders rather than growers.

2 See also EC (1995).

3 See also Gardner (1996, p. 10) and Nello (1997).

4 See Swinbank and Tanner (1996, p. 144) for a set of estimates on food prices.

5 For presentation of a range of estimates on these issues, see Atkin (1995).

6 See Ockenden and Franklin (1995) and Swinbank and Tanner (1996, p. 57).

7 For a survey of the political economy of agriculture, incorporating the shifting incidence of agricultural interests – why does policy tend to shift over time from taxation of agriculture to measures of support? – see Swinnen and van der Zee (1993) and Gardner (1995). Nello (1997) offers a clear exposition in the EU context. See also Gardner (1996). For a debate over the analytical issues involved, see de Gorter and Swinnen (1994 and 1995) and Brooks (1995). For Brooks: 'Weaknesses arise from the fact that they [standard analyses] are inherently deterministic, discounting the importance of historical precedent, institutional structures, cultural values and political leadership' (p. 401). On the latter point Griffiths and Girvin (eds) (1995) observe how functionalist and deterministic is the treatment of the CAP, with simply conceived economic interests readily and directly translated to the political arena and from the national to the international stage. See also Fine et al. (1996, Chapter 2).

8 For a presentation and critique of standard assessments of the impact of the GATT reforms for agriculture, see Walker (1994).

9 For an assessment of the impact of the CAP reform, see Barclay (1993).

10 See Scoppola (1995) for the economic and political role of multinational traders in bulk food commodities.

11 These include two contributions from Swinbank.

12 Considerations and calculations through incorporation of the general equilibrium assessment of such direct and indirect effects, together with assumptions about future policy parameters, have been boosted in the context of agriculture by sophisticated application of the methods involved to the impact of the Uruguay Round. For recent examples, see Sharma et al. (1996) and Harrison et al. (1997). For reference to and critical commentary on earlier literature, see Fine et al. (1996, Chapter 2).

13 See Swann (1995), for example.

14 One indicator that the CAP (and GATT) reform is unconsciously considered to be important in determining what we eat arises when they are considered in a broader context and the longer term. For both Swinbank and Tanner (1996, p. 150) and Gardner (1996, p. 100) acknowledge that the reforms symbolise the first step in a long process of liberalisation – an implicit acceptance of the incorporation of the CAP within the structures of previously regulated markets.

15 Fine et al. (1996, Chapter 7) provides a full critique of the methodology underlying these price calculations, even if not in the context of the CAP. In brief, the price elasticities are calculated on the basis that underlying consumer preferences are given even though the results

themselves indicate major changes in the trends of preferences in the vast majority of cases.

16 Differences across meat systems in the EU have, for example, been symbolised by the mad cow crisis.

17 For consideration of food poverty in the UK context, see Leather (1996) and Dowler (1997).

18 Riska (1993) observes that one factor in the evolution and impact of nutritional science is the extent to which it is dominated as a profession by men or women, as in Finland compared to the United States, respectively.

19 The relationship between the importance of agriculture and the extent to which it receives support is not simple. For, as agriculture declines, it has been able to command adjustment costs, often in the name of national self-sufficiency.

20 See Hill (1992) and also Milio (1990).

21 For an account of such complexity in the context of Sweden, see Vail *et al.* (1994).

22 These illustrations of feedback mechanisms are discussed at length in Fine *et al.* (1996).

23 Other special features of the Norwegian model highlighted are the use of existing health clinics for monitoring the diseases associated with chronically poor diet, the collaboration between nutritionists and doctors, and the involvement of the public.

24 To farmers, low-fat milk has the advantage over full-cream milk of the need to supply more in volume, and also the advantage of potentially mopping up and expanding the demand provided by the less palatable fully skimmed milk.

25 See Figure 4.1 in Chapter 4 for a presentation of the Pyramid and how it diverges from the diet encouraged by food advertising.

26 See also Jensen (1993, 1994) and Kjaernes (1994a).

6 WHITHER FOOD POLICY?

1 An idea of the number and variety of these can be seen from the list of respondents to the James Report (1997) (for further details see pp. 118–20) as listed in Appendix 1 to the White Paper.

2 The subtitle to the White Paper.

3 For a diary of events, see Tansey and Worsley (1995, Appendix 3).

4 There appears to be an acknowledgement of the work of Lang *et al.* (1997).

REFERENCES

Achterberg, C. and K. Clark (1992) 'A Retrospective Examination of Theory Use in Nutrition Education', *Journal of Nutrition Education*, vol. 24, no. 5, pp. 227–33.

Alberto-Fidanza, A. (1990) 'Mediterranean Meal Patterns', in Somogyi and Koskinen (eds) (1990).

Allison, D. and S. Heshka (1993) 'Emotion and Eating in Obesity – A Critical Analysis', *International Journal of Eating Disorders*, vol. 13, no. 3, pp. 289–95.

Andersen, A. and L. Didomenico (1992) 'Diet vs Shape Content of Popular Male and Female Magazines – A Dose–Response Relationship to the Incidence of Eating Disorders', *International Journal of Eating Disorders*, vol. 11, no. 3, pp. 283–7.

Anderson, A. *et al.* (1988) 'Nutrition Knowledge Assessed by a Structured Questionnaire in a Group of Medical In-Patients', *Journal of Human Nutrition and Dietetics*, vol. 1, pp. 39–46.

Anderson, E. (1988) *The Food of China*, New Haven: Yale University Press.

Andrews, B. (1997) 'Bodily Shame in Relation to Abuse in Childhood and Bulimia: A Preliminary Investigation', *British Journal of Clinical Psychology*, vol. 36, no. 1, pp. 41–50.

Andrews, B. *et al.* (1995) 'Depression and Eating Disorders Following Abuse in Childhood in Two Generations of Women', *British Journal of Clinical Psychology*, vol. 34, no. 1, pp. 37–52.

Apte, M. and J. Katona-Apte (1986) 'Diet and Social Movements in American Society: The Last Two Decades', in Fenton and Kisban (eds) (1986).

Arnott, M. (ed.) (1975) *Gastronomy: The Anthropology of Food and Food Habits*, The Hague: Mouton Press.

Artis, M. and N. Lee (eds) (1994) *The Economics of the European Union: Policy and Analysis*, Oxford: Oxford University Press.

Ashwell, M. (1992) 'Nutrition Communication – The Scientist's View', in Buttriss (ed.) (1992).

Atkin, M. (1995) *Snouts in the Trough: European Farmers, the Common Agricultural Policy and the Public Purse*, Cambridge: Woodhead Publishing.

Auld, G. *et al.* (1994) 'Misconceptions about Fats and Cholesterol – Implications for Dietary Guidelines', *Ecology of Food and Nutrition*, vol. 33, no. 1–2, pp. 15–25.

Axelson, M. and D. Brinberg (1992) 'The Measurement and Conceptualization of Nutrition Knowledge', *Journal of Nutrition Education*, vol. 24, no. 5, pp. 239–46.

Bailey, W. and T. Hamilton (1992) 'Feminism and Anorectic Tendencies in College-Women', *Psychological Reports*, vol. 71, no. 3, part 1, pp. 957–8.

Banks, C. (1997) 'The Imaginative Use of Religious Symbols in Subjective Experience of Anorexia Nervosa', *Psychoanalytic Review*, vol. 84, no. 2, pp. 227–36.

Barclay, C. (1993) *The Common Agricultural Policy One Year After Reform*, House of Commons Library, Research Paper, no. 93/74.

Barker, L. (ed.) (1982) *The Psychobiology of Human Food Selection*, Chichester: Ellis Horwood.

Beardsworth, A. and T. Keil (1992) 'The Vegetarian Option – Varieties, Conversions, Motives and Careers', *Sociological Review*, vol. 40, no. 2, pp. 253–93.

Beardsworth, A. and T. Keil (1997) *Sociology on the Menu: An Invitation to the Study of Food and Society*, London: Routledge.

Beebe, D. *et al.* (1996) 'Is Body Focus Restricted to Self-Evaluation? Body Focus in the Evaluation of Self and Others', vol. 20, no. 4, pp. 415–22.

Beggs, L. *et al.* (1993) 'Tracking Nutrition Trends – Canadians' Attitudes, Knowledge and Behaviors Regarding Fat, Fiber and Cholesterol', *Journal of the Canadian Dietic Association*, vol. 54, no. 1, pp. 21–5.

Belasco, W. (1989) *Appetite for Change: How the Counterculture Took on the Food Industry, 1966–1988*, New York: Pantheon.

Bemporad, J. (1996) 'Self-Starvation Through the Ages: Reflections of the Pre-History of Anorexia Nervosa', *International Journal of Eating Disorders*, vol. 19, no. 3, pp. 217–37.

Bennett, P. *et al.* (1994) 'Health Locus of Control and Value for Health as Predictors of Dietary Behavior', *Psychology and Health*, vol. 10, no. 1, pp. 41–54.

Beumont, P. (1995) 'The Clinical Presentation of Anorexia and Bulimia Nervosa', in Brownell and Fairbairn (eds) (1995).

Biener, L. and A. Heaton (1995) 'Women Dieters of Normal Weight: Their Motives, Goals, and Risks', *American Journal of Public Health*, vol. 85, no. 5, May, pp. 714–17.

Black, A. and M. Rayner (1992) *Just Read the Label: Understanding Nutrition Information in Numeric, Verbal and Graphic Formats*, London: HMSO.

Blaxter, K. and N. Robertson (1995) *From Dearth to Plenty: The Modern Revolution in Food Production*, Cambridge: Cambridge University Press.

Bleau, R. (1996) 'Dietary Restraint and Anxiety in Adolescent Girls', *British Journal of Clinical Psychology*, vol. 35, no. 4, pp. 573–84.

Blundell, R. (1988) 'Consumer Behaviour: Theory and Empirical Evidence – A Survey', *Economic Journal*, vol. 98, March, pp. 16–65.

BNF, DHSS, HEC (1977) *Nutrition Education: Report of a Working Party*, London: HMSO.

REFERENCES

Bogin, B. (1991) 'The Evolution of Human Nutrition', in Romanucci-Ross *et al.* (eds) (1991).

Bonanno, A. *et al.* (1995) 'Global Agro-Food Corporations and the State: The Ferruzzi Case', *Rural Sociology*, vol. 60, no. 2, pp. 274–96.

Bordo, S. (1990) 'Reading the Slender Body', in Jacobus *et al.* (eds) (1990).

Bordo, S. (1993) *Unbearable Weight: Feminism, Western Culture, and the Body*, Berkeley: University of California Press.

Bowyer, C. (1988) 'Dietary Factors in Eating Disorders', in Scott (ed.) (1988).

Bradby, H. (1997) 'Health, Eating and Heart Attacks: Glaswegian Punjabi Women's Thinking about Everyday Food', in Caplan (ed.) (1997).

Brandtzaeg, B. and U. Kjaernes (1987) 'Nutrition Policy Problems in an Economy of Plenty', *World Health Forum*, vol. 8, no. 4, pp. 533–8.

Bray, A. (1996) 'The Anorexic Body: Reading Disorders', *Cultural Studies*, vol. 10, no. 3, pp. 413–29.

Brooks, J. (1995) 'The Economic Polity of Farm Policy: Comment', *Journal of Agricultural Economics*, vol. 46, no. 3, Sept., pp. 398–402.

Brown, A. and A. Deaton (1972) 'Surveys in Applied Economics: Models of Consumer Behaviour', *Economic Journal*, vol. 82, Dec., pp. 1145–236.

Brownell, K. (1995) 'History of Obeisty', in Brownell and Fairbairn (eds) (1995).

Brownell, K. and C. Fairbairn (eds) (1995) *Eating Disorders and Obesity: A Comprehensive Handbook*, London: Guilford Press.

Brownell, K. and J. Rodin (1994) 'The Dieting Maelstrom – Is It Possible and Advisable to Lose Weight?', *American Psychologist*, vol. 49, no. 9, pp. 781–91.

Brownell, K. and T. Wadden (1992) 'Etiology and Treatment of Obesity – Understanding a Serious, Prevalent, and Refractory Disorder', *Journal of Consulting and Clinical Psychology*, vol. 60, no. 4, pp. 505–17.

Brumberg, J. (1988) *Fasting Girls: The Emergence of Anorexia Nervosa as a Modern Disease*, Cambridge, MA: Harvard University Press.

Brumberg, J. (1992) 'From Psychiatric Syndrome to "Communicable" Disease: The Case of Anorexia Nervosa', in Rosen (ed.) (1992).

Bryant-Waugh, R. and B. Lask (1995) 'Eating Disorders – An Overview', *Journal of Family Therapy*, vol. 17, no. 1, pp. 13–30.

Budd, J. and R. McCron (1982) *The Role of the Mass Media in Health Education*, University of Leicester: Centre for Mass Communication Research.

Burghardt, R. (1990) 'The Cultural Context of Diet, Disease and the Body', in Harrison and Waterlow (eds) (1990).

Burkitt, D. (1994) 'The Emergence of a Concept', in Temple and Burkitt (eds) (1994).

Burnett, J. and D. Oddy (eds) (1994) *The Origins and Development of Food Policies in Europe*, Leicester: Leicester University Press.

Butler, N. (1988) 'An Overview of Anorexia Nervosa', in Scott (ed.) (1988).

Button, E. *et al.* (1996) 'A Prospective Study of Self-Esteem in the Prediction of Eating Problems in Adolescent Schoolgirls: Questionnaire Findings', *British Journal of Clinical Psychology*, vol. 35, no. 2, pp. 193–203.

REFERENCES

Buttriss, J. (ed.) (1992) *Getting the Messages Across: Nutrition and Communication*, London: National Dairy Council.
Calam, R. and P. Slade (1994) 'Eating Patterns and Unwanted Sexual Experiences', in Dolan and Gittinger (eds) (1994).
Calnan, M. and S. Williams (1991) 'Style of Life and the Salience of Health: An Explanatory Study of Health-Related Practices in Households from Differing Socioeconomic Circumstances', *Sociology of Health and Illness*, vol. 13, no. 4, pp. 506–29.
Campbell, P. (1995) 'What Would a Causal Explanation of the Eating Disorders Look Like?', in Szmukler *et al.* (eds) (1995).
Campbell, T. and T. O'Connor (1988) 'Scientific Evidence and Explicit Health Claims in Food Advertisements', *Journal of Nutrition Education*, vol. 20, no. 2, pp. 87–92.
Cannon, G. (1992) *Food and Health: The Experts Agree. An Analysis of One Hundred Authoritative Scientific Reports on Food, Nutrition and Public Health Published Throughout the World in Thirty Years, between 1961 and 1991*, London: Consumers' Association.
Caplan, P. (1997) 'Approaches to the Study of Food, Health and Identity', in Caplan (ed.) (1997).
Caplan, P. (ed.) (1997) *Food, Health and Identity*, London: Routledge.
Card, M. and C. Freeman (1996) 'The Dismantling of a Myth: A Review of Eating Disorders and Socioeconomic Status', *International Journal of Eating Disorders*, vol. 20, no. 1, pp. 1–12.
Carrier, J. and D. Miller (eds) (1998) *Virtualism: The New Political Economy*, London: Berg.
Cash, T. and E. Deagle (1997) 'The Nature and Extent of Body-Image Disturbances in Anorexia Nervosa and Bulimia Nervosa: A Meta-Analysis', *International Journal of Eating Disorders*, vol. 22, no. 2, pp. 107–26.
Casper, R. (1983) 'On the Emergence of Bulimia Nervosa as a Syndrome', *International Journal of Eating Disorders*, vol. 2, no. 3, pp. 3–16.
Casson, M. (1994) 'Brands: Economic Ideology and Consumer Society', in Jones and Morgan (eds) (1994).
Caswell, J. and D. Padberg (1992) 'Toward a More Comprehensive Theory of Food Labels', *American Journal of Agricultural Economics*, vol. 74, no. 2, pp. 460–8
Cawley, D. *et al.* (1994) 'The Common Agricultural Policy and the UK Diet', paper presented to the 36th Seminar of the European Association of Agricultural Economists, Reading, September.
Chapman, G. and H. MacLean (1993) ' "Junk Food" and "Healthy Food": Meanings of Food in Adolescent Women's Culture', *Journal of Nutrition Education*, vol. 25, no. 3, pp. 102–7.
Charles, N. and M. Kerr (1988) *Women, Food and Families*, Manchester: Manchester University Press.
Chernin, K. (1986) *The Hungry Self: Women, Eating and Identity*, London: Virago.
Colditz, G. (1992) 'Economic Costs of Obesity', *American Journal of Clinical Nutrition*, vol. 55, no. 2, pp. S503–7.
Cole-Hamilton, I. *et al.* (1986) 'A Study Among Dietitians and Adult Members of Their Households of the Practicalities and Implications of

Following Proposed Dietary Guidelines for the UK', *Human Nutrition: Applied Nutrition*, vol. 40A, pp. 365–89.

Coles, A. and S. Turner (1995) *Diet and Health in School Age Children*, London: HEA.

Colman, D. and D. Roberts (1994) 'The Common Agricultural Policy', in Artis and Lee (eds) (1994).

COMA (1984) *Report of Advisory Panel on Diet in Relation to Cardiovascular Disease*, Committee on Medical Aspects of Food Policy, London: HMSO.

Consumers International (1996) *A Spoonful of Sugar. Television Advertising Aimed at Children: An International Comparative Survey*, London: Consumers International.

Cooper, C. (1997) 'Can a Fat Woman Call Herself Disabled?', *Disability and Society*, vol. 12, no. 1, pp. 31–42.

Cosford, P. and E. Arnold (1992) 'Eating Disorders in Later Life – A Review', *International Journal of Geriatric Psychiatry*, vol. 7, no. 7, pp. 491–8.

Crago, M. *et al.* (1996) 'Eating Disturbances Among American Minority Groups: A Review', *International Journal of Eating Disorders*, vol. 19, no. 3, pp. 239–48.

Crandall, C. (1995) 'Do Parents Discriminate against Their Heavyweight Daughters?', *Personality and Social Psychology Bulletin*, vol. 21, no. 7, pp. 724–35.

Cremer, S. and L. Kessler (1992) 'The Fat and Fiber Content of Foods – What Americans Know', *Journal of Nutrition Education*, vol. 24, no. 3, pp. 149–52.

Dansky, B. *et al.* (1997) 'The National Women's Study: Relationship of Victimization and Post-Traumatic Stress Disorder to Bulimia Nervosa', *International Journal of Eating Disorders*, vol. 21, no. 3, pp. 213–28.

Davis, C. and J. Yager (1992) 'Transcultural Aspects of Eating Disorders: A Critical Literature Review', *Culture, Medicine and Psychiatry*, vol. 16, no. 3, Sept., pp. 377–94.

Davison, C. *et al.* (1991) 'Lay Epidemiology and the Prevention Paradox: The Implications of Coronary Candidacy for Health Education', *Sociology of Health and Illness*, vol. 13, no. 1, pp. 1–19.

Deaton, A. and J. Muellbauer (1980) *Economics and Consumer Behaviour*, Cambridge: Cambridge University Press.

de Gorter, H. and J. Swinnen (1994) 'The Economic Polity of Farm Policy', *Journal of Agricultural Economics*, vol. 45, no. 3, Sept., pp. 312–26.

de Gorter, H. and J. Swinnen (1995) 'The Economic Polity of Farm Policy: Reply', *Journal of Agricultural Economics*, vol. 46, no. 3, Sept., pp. 403–14.

Delahoyde, M. and S. Despenich (1994) 'Creating Meat-Eaters: The Child as Advertising Target', *Journal of Popular Culture*, vol. 28, no. 1, pp. 135–50.

den Hartog, A. *et al.* (eds) (1994) *Food Technology, Science, and Marketing: The European Diet in the Twentieth Century*, Edinburgh: Canongate Academic.

Devine, C. and C. Olson (1992) 'Women's Perceptions about the Way Social Roles Promote or Constrain Personal Nutrition Care', *Women and Health*, vol. 19, no. 1, pp. 79–95.

Dietz, T. *et al.* (1995) 'Values and Vegetarianism: An Exploratory Analysis', *Rural Sociology*, vol. 60, no. 3, pp. 533–42.

Doan, R. and L. Bisharat (1990) 'Female Autonomy and Child Nutritional Status: The Extended-Family Residential Unit in Amman', *Social Science and Medicine*, vol. 31, no. 7, pp. 783–9.

Dolan, B. and I. Gittinger (eds) (1994) *Why Women? Gender Issues and Eating Disorders*, London: Athlone Press.

Domel, S. *et al.* (1993) 'Measuring Fruit and Vegetable Preferences among 4th-Grade and 5th-Grade Students', *Preventive Medicine*, vol. 22, no. 6, pp. 866–79.

Douglas, M. and J. Gross (1981) 'Food and Culture: Measuring the Intricacy of Rule Systems', *Social Science Information*, vol. 20, no. 1, pp. 1–35.

Dowler, E. (1997) 'Budgeting for Food on Low Income in the UK: The Case of Lone-Parent Families', *Food Policy*, vol. 22, no. 5, pp. 405–17.

Dyson, T. (1996) *Population and Food: Global Trends and Future Prospects*, London: Routledge.

Eatwell, J. *et al.* (eds) (1987) *The New Palgrave: A Dictionary of Economics*, London: Macmillan.

EC (1995) *The Agricultural Situation in the European Union: 1994 Report*, Luxembourg: European Commission.

Emmons, L. (1992) 'Dieting and Purging Behavior in Black and White High School Students', *Journal of the American Dietetic Assocation*, vol. 92, no. 3, pp. 306–12.

Esler, I. (1995) 'Family Models of Eating Disorders', in Szmukler *et al.* (eds) (1995).

Falk, P. (1991) '*Homo Culinarius*: Towards an Historical Anthropology of Taste', *Social Science Information*, vol. 30, no. 4, pp. 757–90.

Fallows, S. and H. Gosden (1985) *Does the Consumer Really Care?*, University of Bradford: Food Policy Research Unit.

Farb, P. and G. Arpelagos (eds) (1983) *Consuming Passions: The Anthropology of Eating*, Boston: Houghton-Mifflin Co.

Fenton, A. and E. Kisban (eds) (1986) *Food in Change: Eating Habits from the Middle Ages to the Present Day*, Edinburgh: John Donald Publishers.

Fiddes, N. (1991) *Meat: A Natural Symbol*, London: Routledge.

Fine, B. (1992) *Women's Employment and the Capitalist Family*, London: Routledge.

Fine, B. (1993) 'Modernity, Urbanism, and Modern Consumption – A Comment', *Environment and Planning D, Society and Space*, vol. 11, pp. 599–601.

Fine, B. (1995a) 'Towards a Political Economy of Anorexia?', *Appetite*, vol. 24, pp. 231–42.

Fine, B. (1995b) 'From Political Economy to Consumption', in Miller (ed.) (1995).

Fine, B. (1997a) 'Entitlement Failure?', *Development and Change*, vol. 28, no. 4, pp. 617–47.

Fine, B. (1997b) 'Playing the Consumption Game', *Consumption, Markets, Culture*, vol. 1, no. 1, pp. 7–29.

Fine, B. (1998a) *Labour Market Theory: A Constructive Reassessment*, London: Routledge.

Fine, B. (1998b) 'The Triumph of Economics: Or "Rationality" Can Be Dangerous to Your Reasoning', in Carrier and Miller (eds) (1999).

Fine, B. and L. Harris (1985) *The Peculiarities of the British Economy*, London: Lawrence and Wishart.

Fine, B. and C. Lapavitsas (1998) 'Markets and Money in Social Theory: What Role for Economics?', mimeo.

Fine, B. and E. Leopold (1993) *The World of Consumption*, London: Routledge.

Fine, B. and J. Wright (1991) 'Digesting the Food and Information Systems', *Birkbeck Discussion Paper*, no. 7/91, Dec.

Fine, B. *et al.* (1996) *Consumption in the Age of Affluence: The World of Food*, London: Routledge.

Fine, B. *et al.* (1998) 'What We Eat and Why: A Socioeconomic Approach to Standard Items in Food Consumption', in Murcott (ed.) (1998).

Fischler, C. (1980) 'Food Habits, Social Change and the Nature/Culture Dilemma', *Social Science Information*, vol. 19, no. 6, pp. 937–53.

Fischler, C. (1988) 'Food, Self and Identity', *Social Science Information*, vol. 27, no. 2, pp. 275–92.

Fischler, C. (1989) 'Cuisines and Food Selection', in Thomson (ed.) (1989).

Foster, G. and F. Kaferstein (1985) 'Food Safety and the Behaviourial Sciences', *Social Science and Medicine*, vol. 21, no. 11, pp. 1273–7.

Frederick, C. and V. Grow (1996) 'A Mediational Model of Autonomy, Self-Esteem, and Eating Disordered Attitudes and Behaviors', *Psychology of Women Quarterly*, vol. 20, no. 2, pp. 217–28.

French, J. and L. Adams (1986) 'From Analysis to Synthesis: Theories of Health Education', *Health Education Journal*, vol. 45, no. 2, pp. 71–4.

French, S. and R. Jeffery (1994) 'Consequences of Dieting to Lose Weight – Effects on Physical and Mental Health', *Health Psychology*, vol. 13, no. 3, pp. 195–212.

French, S. *et al.* (1995) 'Frequent Dieting among Adolescents: Psychosocial and Health Behavior Correlates', *American Journal of Public Health*, vol. 85, no. 5, May, pp. 695–701.

French, S. *et al.* (1996) 'Sexual Orientation and Prevalence of Body Dissatisfaction and Eating Disordered Behaviors: A Population-Based Study of Adolescents', *International Journal of Eating Disorders*, vol. 19, no. 2, pp. 119–26.

Frewer, L. *et al.* (1994) 'The Interrelationship between Perceived Knowledge, Control and Risk Associated with a Range of Food-Related Hazards Targeted at the Individual, Other People and Society', *Journal of Food Safety*, vol. 14, no. 1, pp. 19–40.

Friedman, M. and K. Brownell (1995) 'Psychological Correlates of Obesity: Moving to the Next Research Generation', *Psychological Bulletin*, vol. 117, no. 1, pp. 3–20.

Furnham, A. and R. Patel (1994) 'The Eating Attitudes and Behaviours of Asian and British School Girls: A Pilot Study', *International Journal of Social Psychiatry*, vol. 40, no. 3, pp. 214–26.

Gamman, L. and M. Makinen (1994) *Female Fetishism: A New Look*, London: Lawrence and Wishart.

Gardner, B. (1992) 'Changing Economic Perspectives on the Farm Problem', *Journal of Economic Literature*, vol. XXX, March, pp. 62–101.

Gardner, B. (1995) *Plowing Ground in Washington: The Political Economy of US Agriculture*, San Francisco: Pacific Research Institute for Public Policy.

Gardner, B. (1996) *European Agriculture: Policies, Production and Trade*, London: Routledge.

Garrett, C. (1996) 'Recovery from Anorexia Nervosa: A Durkheimian Interpretation', *Social Science and Medicine*, vol. 43, no. 10, pp. 1489–506.

Garrett, C. (1997) 'Recovery from Anorexia Nervosa: A Sociological Perspective', *International Journal of Eating Disorders*, vol. 21, no. 3, pp. 261–72.

Gibney, M. (1990) 'Dietary Guidelines: A Critical Appraisal', *Journal of Human Nutrition and Dietetics*, vol. 49, no. 3, pp. 245–54.

Gibson, L. *et al.* (1990) 'Evaluation Methodologies for Food Health Policies', *Journal of Human Nutrition and Dietetics*, vol. 3, pp. 55–9.

Gillespie, A. (1987) 'A Survey of Nutritionists' Opinions on Objectives of a Dietary Guidance System', *Journal of Nutrition Education*, vol. 19, no. 5, pp. 220–4.

Gillespie, A. and J. Brun (1992) 'Trends and Challenges for Nutrition Education Research', *Journal of Nutrition Education*, vol. 24, no. 5, pp. 222–6.

Glanz, K. and J. Rudd (1993) 'Views of Theory, Research, and Practice: A Survey of Nutrition Education and Consumer Behavior Professionals', *Journal of Nutrition Education*, vol. 25, no. 5, pp. 269–73.

Glennie, P. and N. Thrift (1992) 'Modernity, Urbanism, and Modern Consumption', *Environment and Planning D: Society and Space*, vol. 10, no. 4, pp. 423–43.

Glennie, P. and N. Thrift (1993) 'Modern Consumption: Theorising Commodities and Consumers', *Environment and Planning D: Society and Space*, vol. 11, pp. 603–6.

Goldberg, J. (1992) 'Nutrition and Health Communication – The Message and the Media', *Nutrition Reviews*, vol. 50, no. 3, pp. 71–7.

Gordon, R. (1990) *Anorexia and Bulimia: Anatomy of a Social Epidemic*, Oxford: Basil Blackwell.

Gormley T. (1987) 'Review and Assessment of Key Nutritional Issues and of the Criteria Currently Applied for Determining the Effects of Food of Plant, Animal and Marine Origin on Human Health', in Gormley *et al.* (1987).

Gormley, T. *et al.* (1987) *Food Health and the Consumer*, London: Elsevier.

Greenberg, D. and D. LaPorte (1996) 'Racial Differences in Body Type Preferences of Men for Women', *International Journal of Eating Disorders*, vol. 19, no. 3, pp. 275–8.

Griffiths, R. and B. Girvin (eds) (1995) *The Green Pool and the Origins of the Common Agricultural Policy*, London: Lothian Press.

Grivetti, L. *et al.* (1987) 'Threads of Cultural Nutrition: Arts and Humanities', *Progress in Food and Nutrition Science*, vol. 11, pp. 249–306.

Guthrie, H. (1978) 'Is Education Not Enough?', *Journal of Nutrition Education*, vol. 10, no. 2, Apr./June, pp. 57–8

Guthrie, J. *et al.* (1995) 'Who Uses Nutrition Labeling, and What Effect Does Label Use Have on Diet Quality?', *Journal of Nutrition Education*, vol. 27, no. 4, pp. 163–72.

Hall, P. and R. Driscoll (1993) 'Anorexia in the Elderly – An Annotation', *International Journal of Eating Disorders*, vol. 14, no. 4, pp. 497–9.

Harper, A. (1989) 'Scientific Substantiation of Health Claims: How Much is Enough?', *Nutrition Today*, Mar./Apr., pp. 17–21.

Harris, M. *et al.* (1984) 'Food Intake in a Multicultural Southwestern Population: Ethnic, Gender and Age Distributions', *Ecology of Food and Nutrition*, vol. 21, pp. 287–96.

Harrison, G. and J. Waterlow (eds) (1990) *Diet and Disease in Traditional and Developing Countries*, Cambridge: Cambridge University Press.

Harrison, G. *et al.* (1997) 'Quantifying the Uruguay Round', *Economic Journal*, vol. 107, no. 444, pp. 1405–30.

Harrison, K. and J. Cantor (1997) 'The Relationship between Media Consumption and Eating Disorders', *Journal of Communication*, vol. 47, no. 1, pp. 40–67.

Harriss, B. (1990) 'Food Distribution, Death and Disease in South Asia', in Harrison and Waterlow (eds) (1990).

Harriss-White, B. and R. Hoffenberg (eds) (1994) *Food: Multidisciplinary Perspectives*, Oxford: Basil Blackwell.

HEA (1989) *Diet, Nutrition and Healthy Eating in Low Income Groups*, London: Health Education Authority.

Heasman, M. (1990) 'Nutrition and Technology: The Development of the Market for "Lite" Products', *British Food Journal*, vol. 92, no. 2, pp. 5–13.

Henderson, L. and P. Vickers (1995) 'Health or Beauty? A Survey of Dundee Women's Attitudes to Body Size', *Health Education Journal*, vol. 54, no. 1, Mar., pp. 61–73.

Hesse-Biber, S. (1996) *Am I Thin Enough Yet? The Cult of Thinness and the Commercialization of Identity*, New York: Oxford University Press.

Hill, A. *et al.* (1992) 'Eating in the Adult World – The Risk of Dieting in Childhood and Adolescence', *British Journal of Clinical Psychology*, vol. 31, no. 1, pp. 95–105.

Hill, B. (1996) *Farm Incomes, Wealth and Agricultural Policy*, Aldershot: Avebury, second edition.

Hill, G. (1995) 'The Impact of Breakfast Especially Ready-to-Eat Cereals on Nutrient Intake and Health of Children', *Nutrition Research*, vol. 15, no. 4, pp. 595–613.

Hill, M. (1992) *The Politics of Dietary Change*, Aldershot: Dartmouth.

Holm, L. (1993) 'Cultural and Social Acceptability of a Healthy Diet', *European Journal of Clinical Nutrition*, vol. 47, no. 8, pp. 592–9.

Holmwood, J. *et al.* (eds) (1994) *Constructing the New Consumer Society*, London: Macmillan.

Honjo, S. (1996) 'A Mother's Complaints of Overeating by Her 25-Month-Old Daughter: A Proposal of Anorexia Nervosa by Proxy', *International Journal of Eating Disorders*, vol. 20, no. 4, pp. 433–7.

Hopwood, C. (1995) 'My Discourse/My-Self: Therapy as Possibility (for Women Who Eat Compulsively)', *Feminist Review*, no. 49, pp. 66–85.

Ippolito, P. and A. Mathios (1989) *Health Claims in Advertising and Labeling: A Study of the Cereal Market*, Washington: Federal Trade Commission.

Ippolito, P. and A. Mathios (1990) 'The Regulation of Science-Based Claims in Advertising', *Journal of Consumer Policy*, vol. 13, Dec., pp. 413–45.

Ippolito, P. and A. Mathios (1993) 'New Food Labeling Regulations and the Flow of Nutrition Information to Consumers', *Journal of Public Policy and Marketing*, vol. 12, no. 2, Fall, pp. 188–205.

Ippolito, P. and A. Mathios (1994a) 'Information, Policy, and the Sources of Fat and Cholesterol in the US Diet', *Journal of Public Policy and Marketing*, vol. 12, no. 2, Fall, pp. 200–17.

Ippolito, P. and A. Mathios (1994b) 'Information and Advertising: The Case of Fat Consumption in the United States', *American Economic Review*, vol. 85, no. 2, May, pp. 91–5.

Ippolito, P. and A. Mathios (1995) 'Nutrition Information and Policy: A Study of US Food Production Trends', *Journal of Consumer Policy*, vol. 17, no. 3, September, pp. 271–305.

Ippolito, P. and A. Mathios (1996) *Information and Advertising Policy: A Study of Fat and Cholesterol Consumption in the United States, 1977–1990*, Washington: Federal Trade Commission.

Jackson, L. (1984) 'Hierarchic Demand and the Engel Curve for Variety', *Review of Economics and Statistics*, vol. 66, no. 1, Feb., pp. 8–15.

Jacobus, M. *et al.* (eds) (1990) *Body/Politics: Women and the Discourse of Sciences*, London: Routledge.

James, P. (1994) 'The Nature of Food: Essential Requirements', in Harriss-White and Hoffenberg (eds) (1994).

James Report (1997) *Food Standards Agency: An Interim Report by Professor Philip James*, mimeo.

Jansen, A. (1996) 'How Restrained Eaters Perceive the Amount They Eat', *British Journal of Clinical Psychology*, vol. 35, no. 3, pp. 381–92.

Jansson, S. (1995) 'Food Practices and Division of Domestic Labor – A Comparison between British and Swedish Households', *Sociological Review*, vol. 43, no. 3, pp. 462–77.

Jarman, M. *et al.* (1997) 'The Psychological Battle for Control: A Qualitative Study of Health-Care Professionals' Understanding of the Treatment of Anorexia Nervosa', *Journal of Community and Applied Social Psychology*, vol. 7, no. 2, pp. 137–52.

Jensen, T. (1993) 'Nutrition: A Dilemma in the Politics of Food', in Kjaernes *et al.* (eds) (1993).

Jensen, T. (1994) 'The Political History of Norwegian Nutrition Policy', in Burnett and Oddy (eds) (1994).

Jensen, T. *et al.* (1986) 'Health, Nutrition and Agriculture Policy: The Norwegian Experience', paper presented to the Annual Meeting of the American Public Health Association, Las Vegas, October.

Jerome, N. (1975) 'On Determining Food Patterns of Urban Dwellers in Contemporary United States Society', in Arnott (ed.) (1975).

Jerome, N. *et al.* (eds) (1980) *Nutritional Anthropology: Contemporary Approaches to Diet and Culture*, Pleasantville, NJ: Redgrave Publishing Co.

Johnson, D. (1973) *World Agriculture in Disarray*, London: Macmillan; second edition, 1991.

Johnson, T. and M. Wilson (1995) 'An Analysis of Weight-Based Discrimination: Obesity as a Disability', *Labor Law Journal*, vol. 46, no. 4, pp. 238–44.

Joiner, T. *et al.* (1995) 'Body Dissatisfaction: A Feature of Bulimia, Depression or Both?', *Journal of Social and Clinical Psychology*, vol. 14, no. 4, pp. 339–56.

Jones, G. and N. Morgan (eds) (1994) *Adding Value: Brands and Marketing in Food and Drink*, London: Routledge.

Jowell, R. *et al.* (eds) (1990) *British Social Attitudes: The Seventh Report*, Aldershot: Gower.

Kandel, R. and G. Pelto (1980) 'The Health Food Movement: Social Revitalization or Alternative Health Maintenance System', in Jerome *et al.* (eds) (1980).

Karagiannis, G. and K. Velentzas (1997) 'Explaining Food Consumption Patterns in Greece', *Journal of Agricultural Economics*, vol. 48, no. 1, pp. 83–92.

Kaufman, B. *et al.* (1996) 'Intervention in an Elite Ballet Scool: An Attempt at Decreasing Eating Disorders and Injury', *Women's Studies International Forum*, vol. 19, no. 5, pp. 545–50.

Keane, A. (1997) 'Too Hard to Swallow? The Palatability of Healthy Eating Advice', in Caplan (ed.) (1997).

Kelder, S. *et al.* (1995) 'Community-Wide Youth Nutrition Education – Long-Term Outcomes of the Minnesota Heart Health-Program', *Health Education Research*, vol. 10, no. 2, pp. 119–31.

Kemm, J. and D. Booth (1992) *Promotion of Healthier Eating: How to Collect and Use Information for Planning, Monitoring and Evaluation*, London: HMSO.

Khandelwal, S. *et al.* (1995) 'Eating Disorders: An Indian Perspective', *International Journal of Social Psychiatry*, vol. 41, no. 2, pp. 132–46.

Kirk, T. (1991) 'Collaboration between the Dietetic Profession and the Food Industry in Health Education – A Discussion Paper', *Journal of Human Nutrition and Dietetics*, vol. 4, pp. 197–207.

Kirk, T. and U. Arens (1988) 'Legislation and Codes of Practice: Nutrition Information in Food Marketing', *British Food Journal*, vol. 90, no. 6, pp. 268–72.

Kirschenbaum, D. and M. Fitzgibbon (1995) 'Controversy about the Treatment of Obesity – Criticisms or Challenges', *Behavior Therapy*, vol. 26, no. 1, pp. 43–68.

Kjaernes, U. (1993a) 'Norwegian Nutrition Policy: New Problems and Yesterday's Solutions?', paper delivered to the XIIth Nordic Conference on Social Medicine, Kuopio, Finland, 16–18 June.

Kjaernes, U. (1993b) 'A Sacred Cow: The Case of Milk in Norwegian Nutrition Policy', in Kjaernes *et al.* (eds) (1993).

Kjaernes, U. (1994a) 'Political Struggle over Scientific Definitions: Nutrition as a Social Problem in Inter-War Norwegian Nutrition Policy', in Maurer and Sobal (eds) (1994).

Kjaernes, U. (1994b) 'Milk: Nutritional Science and Agricultural Development in Norway, 1890–1990', in den Hartog *et al.* (eds) (1994).

Kjaernes, U. and T. Jensen (1994) 'Political Dilemmas of Designing the Good Life – The Case of Nutrition and Social Democracy', in Holmwood *et al.* (eds) (1994).

Kjaernes, U. *et al.* (eds) (1993) *Regulating Markets, Regulating People: On Food and Nutrition Policy*, Oslo: Novus Press.

Kornberg, A. (1976) 'Nutrition and Science', in Walcher *et al.* (eds) (1976).

Kotz, K. and M. Story (1994) 'Food Advertisements during Children's Saturday Morning Television Programming – Are They Consistent with Dietary Recommendations?', *Journal of the American Dietetics Association*, vol. 94, no. 11, pp. 1296–300.

Lahiri, S. (1990) 'A Redefinition of Luxuries, Necessities, and Engel Goods: An Analysis of Household Budget Data', *Journal of Developing Areas*, vol. 25, no. 1, Oct., pp. 49–67.

Lane, S. (1995) 'The United States Food Policy', *American Journal of Agricultural Economics*, vol. 77, no. 5, pp. 1096–109.

Lang, T. (1986/7) 'The New Food Policies', *Critical Social Policy*, vol. 18, Winter, pp. 32–47.

Lang, T. *et al.* (1997) *Food Standards and the State: A Fresh Start*, Centre for Food Policy, Discussion Paper No. 3, London: Thames Valley University.

Lask, B. and R. Bryant-Waugh (eds) (1993) *Childhood Onset of Anorexia Nervosa and Related Eating Disorders*, Hove: Lawrence Erlbaum Associates.

Leachwood, P. (1990) 'Dieting and Lifestyle', in Somogyi and Koskinen (eds) (1990).

Leather, S. (1996) *The Making of Modern Malnutrition: An Overview of Food Poverty in the UK*, London: Caroline Walker Trust.

Lee, S. (1995) 'Self-Starvation in Context: Towards a Culturally Sensitive Understanding of Anorexia Nervosa', *Social Science and Medicine*, vol. 41, no. 1, pp. 25–36.

Lee, S. (1996) 'Reconsidering the Status of Anorexia Nervosa as a Western Culture-Bound Syndrome', *Social Science and Medicine*, vol. 42, no. 1, pp. 21–34.

Lefebvre, R. *et al.* (1995) 'Social Marketing and Nutrition Education: Inappropriate or Misunderstood?', *Journal of Nutrition Education*, vol. 27, no. 3, pp. 146–50.

Lester, R. (1995) 'Embodied Voices: Women's Food Asceticism and the Negotiation of Identity', *Ethos*, vol. 23, no. 2, pp. 187–222.

Levy, A. *et al.* (1993) 'Nutrition Knowledge Levels about Dietary Fats and Cholesterol: 1983–88', *Journal of Nutrition Education*, vol. 25, no. 2, pp. 60–6

Lieberman, S. (1995) 'Anorexia Nervosa: The Tyranny of Appearances', *Journal of Family Therapy*, vol. 17, no. 1, pp. 133–8.

Lien, M. (1995) 'Fuel for the Body – Nourishment for Dreams: Contradictory Roles of Food in Contemporary Norwegian Food Advertising', *Journal of Consumer Policy*, vol. 18, no. 2–3, pp. 157–86.

Lobstein, T. (1990) 'The Corporate Clinic', *The Food Magazine*, Oct./Dec., pp. 22–3.

Lowe, M. (1995) 'From Robust Appetites to Calorie Counting: The Emergence of Dieting among Smith College Students in the 1920s', *Journal of Women's History*, vol. 7, no. 4, pp. 37–61.

Lupton, D. (1996) *Food, the Body and Self*, London: Sage.

McCluney, J. (1988) *Answering Back: Public Views on Food and Health Information*, University of Bradford: Food Policy Research Unit.

Macdiarmid, J. and M. Hetherington (1995) 'Mood Modulation by Food: An Exploration of Affect and Cravings in "Chocolate Addicts"', *British Journal of Clinical Psychology*, vol. 34, no. 1, pp. 129–38.

McKie, L. and R. Wood (1991) 'Dietary Beliefs and Practices: A Study of Working-Class Women in North-East England', *British Food Journal*, vol. 93, no. 4, pp. 25–8.

McKie, L. *et al.* (1993) 'Women Defining Health – Food, Diet and Body-Image', *Health Education Research*, vol. 8, no. 1, pp. 35–41.

McManus, K. (1990) 'What Can and What Cannot be Achieved by Nutrition Education? A Challenge for the 1990s', *Proceedings of the Nutrition Society*, vol. 49, pp. 389–95.

McNay, L. (ed.) (1992) *Foucault and Feminism: Power, Gender and the Self*, London: Polity Press.

MacSween, M. (1993) *Anorexic Bodies: A Feminist and Sociological Perspective on Anorexia Nervosa*, London: Routledge.

MAFF (1987) *The Use of the Word 'Natural' and Its Derivatives in the Labelling, Advertising and Presentation of Food: Report of a Survey by the Local Authorities Co-ordinating Body on Trading Standards*, London: HMSO.

MAFF (1998) *The Food Standards Agency: A Force for Change*, Cm 3830, London: HMSO.

Malson, H. (1998) *The Thin Woman: Feminism, Post-Structuralism and the Social Psychology of Anorexia Nervosa*, London: Routledge.

Manderson, L. (1987) 'Hot–Cold Food and Medical Theories: Overview and Introduction', *Social Science and Medicine*, vol. 25, no. 4, pp. 329–30.

Martz, D. *et al.* (1995) 'The Relationship between Feminine Gender Role Stress, Body Image, and Eating Disorders', *Psychology of Women Quarterly*, vol. 19, no. 4, pp. 493–508.

Maurer, D. and J. Sobal (eds) (1994) *Eating Agendas: Food and Nutrition as Social Problems*, New York: Aldine de Gruyter.

Mayhew, M. (1988) 'The 1930s Nutrition Controversy', *Journal of Contemporary History*, vol. 23, pp. 445–64.

Meehan, J. (ed.) (1995) *Feminists Read Habermas: Gendering the Subject of Discourse*, London: Routledge.

Mennell, S. (1987) 'On the Civilizing of Appetite', *Theory, Culture and Society*, vol. 4, no. 3, pp. 373–403.

Mennell, S. *et al.* (1992) *The Sociology of Food: Eating, Diet and Culture*, London: Sage, reproduction of the special issue of *Current Sociology*, vol. 40, no. 2.

Merton, R. (1957) *Social Theory and Social Structure*, New York: Free Press.

Milio, N. (1990) *Nutrition Policy for Food-Rich Countries: A Strategic Analysis*, Baltimore: Johns Hopkins University Press.

Miller, C. *et al.* (1995) 'Do Obese Women Have Poorer Social Relationships Than Non-Obese Women? Reports by Self, Friends, and Coworkers', *Journal of Personality*, vol. 63, no. 1, pp. 65–86.

Miller, D. (ed.) (1995) *Acknowledging Consumption*, London: Routledge.

Miller, D. and J. Reilly (1994) 'Making an Issue of Food Safety: The Media, Pressure Groups, and the Public Sphere', in Maurer and Sobal (eds) (1994).

Mills, C.W. (1959) *The Sociological Imagination*, New York: Oxford University Press.

Mills, J. (1995) 'A Note on Interpersonal Sensitivity and Psychotic Symptomatology in Obese Adult-Outpatients with a History of Childhood Obesity', *Journal of Psychology*, vol. 129, no. 3, pp. 345–8.

Mooney, C. (1990) 'Cost and Availability of Healthy Food Choices in a London Health District', *Journal of Human Nutrition and Dietetics*, vol. 3, pp. 111–20.

Morley, D. (1995) 'Theories of Consumption in Media Studies', in Miller (ed.) (1995).

Moyer, P. (1997) 'Childhood Sexual Abuse and Precursors of Binge Eating in an Adolescent Female Population', *International Journal of Eating Disorders*, vol. 21, no. 1, pp. 23–30.

Murcott, A. (1997) 'Family Meals – A Thing of the Past?', in Caplan (ed.) (1997).

Murcott, A. (ed.) (1998) *The Nation's Diet: The Social Science of Food Choice*, New York: Longman.

Murnen, S. and L. Smolak (1997) 'Femininity, Masculinity, and Disordered Eating: A Meta-Analytic Review', *International Journal of Eating Disorders*, vol. 22, no. 3, pp. 231–42.

Murphy, A. *et al.* (1995) 'Kindergarten Students' Food Preferences Are Not Consistent with Their Knowledge of the Dietary Guidelines', *Journal of the American Dietetic Association*, vol. 95, no. 2, pp. 219–23.

Musaiger, A. (1985) 'Can Nutrition Education Compete with Advertising Messages in Developing Countries?', in Turner and Ingle (eds) (1985).

Myers, P. and F. Biocca (1992) 'The Elastic Body Image: The Effect of Television Advertising and Programming on Body Image Distortions in Young Women', *Journal of Communication*, vol. 42, no. 3, Summer, pp. 108–33.

NACNE (1983) *Proposals for Nutritional Guidelines for Health Education in Britain*, National Advisory Committee on Nutrition Education, London: Health Education Authority.

Naik, N. and M. Moore (1996) 'Habit Formation and Intertemporal Substitution in Individual Food Consumption', *Review of Economics and Statistics*, vol. LXXVIII, no. 2, pp. 321–8.

Nello, S. (1997) 'Applying the New Political Economy Approach to Agricultural Policy Formation in the European Union', European University Institute, EUI Working Papers, Robert Schuman Centre, RSC no. 97/21.

Nestle, M. (1993) 'Food Lobbies, the Food Pyramid, and US Nutrition Policy', *International Journal of Health Services*, vol. 23, no. 3, pp. 483–96.

Nestle, M. (1994) 'Traditional Models of Healthy Eating: Alternatives to "Techno-Food"', *Journal of Nutrition Education*, vol. 26, no. 5, pp. 241–5.

Nichols, S. *et al*. (1988) 'Evaluation of the Effectiveness of a Nutritional Health Education Leaflet in Changing Public Knowledge and Attitudes about Eating and Health', *Journal of Human Nutrition and Dietetics*, vol. 1, pp. 233–8.

Nixon, R. (1996) 'The Corporate Assault on the Food and Drug Administration', *International Journal of Health Services*, vol. 26, no. 3, pp. 561–8.

Ockenden, J. and M. Franklin (1995) *European Agriculture: Making the CAP Fit the Future*, London: Royal Institute of International Affairs.

O'Connor, E. (1995) 'Pictures of Health: Medical Photography and the Emergence of Anorexia Nervosa', *Journal of the History of Sexuality*, vol. 5, no. 4, Apr., pp. 535–72.

Orbach, S. (1993) *Hunger Strike: The Anorectic's Struggle as a Metaphor for Our Age*, Harmondsworth: Penguin.

Parker, S. *et al*. (1995) 'Body-Image and Weight Concerns among African-American and White Adolescent Females – Differences That Make a Difference', *Human Organization*, vol. 54, no. 2, pp. 103–14.

Parry-Jones, B. and W. Parry-Jones (1995) 'History of Bulimia and Bulimia Nervosa', in Brownell and Fairbairn (eds) (1995).

Pelto, G. (1987) 'Cultural Issues in Maternal and Child Health and Nutrition', *Social Science and Medicine*, vol. 25, no. 6, pp. 553–9.

Pelto, G. and P. Pelto (1985) 'Diet and Delocalisation: Dietary Changes since 1750', in Rotberg and Rabb (eds) (1985).

Pelto, G. and L. Vargas (1992) 'Introduction: Dietary Change and Nutrition', *Ecology, Food and Nutrition*, vol. 27, no. 3–4, pp. 159–61.

Pelto, P. and G. Pelto (1983) 'Culture, Nutrition, and Health', in Romanucci-Ross *et al*. (eds) (1983).

Pike, K. (1995) 'Bulimic Symptomatology in High School Girls: Toward a Model of Cumulative Risk', *Psychology of Women Quarterly*, vol. 19, no. 3, pp. 373–96.

Pill, R. and N. Stott (1982) 'Concepts of Illness Causation and Responsibility: Some Preliminary Data from a Sample of Working Class Mothers', *Social Science and Medicine*, vol. 16, pp. 43–52.

Polusny, M. and V. Follette (1995) 'Long-Term Correlates of Child Sexual Abuse – Theory and Review of the Empirical Literature', *Applied and Preventive Psychology*, vol. 4, no. 3, pp. 143–66.

Popkin, B. and M. Lim-Ybanez (1982) 'Nutrition and School Achievement', *Social Science and Medicine*, vol. 16, pp. 53–61.

Powell, A. and A. Kahn (1995) 'Racial Differences in Women's Desires to Be Thin', *International Journal of Eating Disorders*, vol. 17, no. 2, pp. 191–5.

Pritchard, W. (1996) 'Shifts in Food Regimes, Regulation, and Producer Cooperatives: Insights from the Australian and US Dairy Industries', *Environment and Planning A*, vol. 28, no. 5, pp. 857–76.

Reid, D. and S. Hendricks (1993) 'Consumer Awareness of Nutrition Information on Food Package Labels', *Journal of the Canadian Dietetic Association*, vol. 54, no. 3, pp. 127–31.

Reilly, J. and D. Miller (1997) 'Scaremonger or Scapegoat? The Role of the Media in the Emergence of Food as a Social Issue', in Caplan (ed.) (1997).

Rennie, D. (1995) 'Health-Education Models and Food Hygiene Education', *Journal of the Royal Society of Health*, vol. 115, no. 2, pp. 75–9.

Richardson, D. (1990) 'Acceptance of Novel Foods in the Market', in Somogyi and Koskinen (eds) (1990).

Richardson, N. *et al.* (1994) 'Meat Consumption, Definition of Meat and Trust in Information Sources in the UK Population and Members of the Vegetarian Society', *Ecology of Food and Nutrition*, vol. 33, no. 1–2, pp. 1–13.

Riska, E. (1993) 'The Gendered Character of Professions in the Field of Nutrition', in Kjaernes *et al.* (eds) (1993).

Ritson, C. (1991) 'The CAP and the Consumer', in Ritson and Harvey (eds) (1991).

Ritson, C. and D. Harvey (eds) (1991) *The Common Agricultural Policy and the World Economy: Essays in Honour of John Ashton*, Wallingford: CAB International.

Robbins, C. (1983) 'Implementing the NACNE Report, National Dietary Goals: A Confused Debate', *The Lancet*, 10 Dec., pp. 1351–3.

Roberts, D. (1991) ' "Natural": A Trading Standards Viewpoint', *British Food Journal*, vol. 93, no. 1, pp. 17–19.

Robinson, T. *et al.* (1993) 'Does Television Viewing Increase Obesity and Reduce Physical-Activity? Cross-Sectional and Longitudinal Analyses Among Adolescent Girls', *Pediatrics*, vol. 91, no. 2, pp. 273–80.

Robison, J. *et al.* (1993) 'Obesity, Weight-Loss, and Health', *Journal of the American Dietetic Association*, vol. 93, no. 4, pp. 445–9.

Rock, I. (ed.) (1990) *The Legacy of Solomon Asch*, Hillsdale, NJ: Lawrence Erlbaum Associates.

Rodgers, A. *et al.* (1994) 'Eat for Health – A Supermarket Intervention for Nutrition and Cancer Risk Reduction', *American Journal of Public Health*, vol. 84, no. 1, pp. 72–6.

Rogers, L. *et al.* (1997) 'The Relationship Between Socioeconomic Status and Eating-Disordered Behaviors in a Community Sample of Adolescent Girls', *International Journal of Eating Disorders*, vol. 22, no. 4, pp. 15–25.

Rolland, K. *et al.* (1997) 'Body Figure Perceptions and Eating Attitudes Among Australian Schoolchildren Aged 8 to 12 Years', *International Journal of Eating Disorders*, vol. 21, no. 3, pp. 273–8.

Romanucci-Ross, L. *et al.* (eds) (1983) *The Anthropology of Medicine: From Culture to Cuisine*, New York: Praeger.

Romanucci-Ross, L. *et al.* (eds) (1991) *The Anthropology of Medicine: From Culture to Method*, New York: Bergin and Harvey.

Romeo, F. (1986) *Understanding Anorexia Nervosa*, Springfield, IL: Charles C. Thomas.

Rosen, C. (ed.) (1992) *Framing Disease: Studies in Cultural History*, New Brunswick, NJ: Rutgers University Press.

Rosen, J. *et al.* (1986) 'Binge-Eating Episodes in Bulimia Nervosa: The Amount and Type of Food Consumed', *International Journal of Eating Disorders*, vol. 5, no. 2, Feb., pp. 255–68.

Rotberg, R. and T. Rabb (eds) (1985) *Hunger and History: The Impact of Changing Food and Production Patterns on Society*, Cambridge: Cambridge University Press.

Rothblum, E. (1990) 'Women and Weight: Fad and Fiction', *Journal of Psychology*, vol. 124, no. 1, pp. 5–24.

Rothblum, E. (1992) 'The Stigma of Women's Weight – Social and Economic Realities', *Feminism and Psychology*, vol. 2, no. 1, pp. 61–73.

Rozin, P. (1982) 'Human Food Selection: The Interaction of Biology, Culture and Individual Experience', in Barker (ed.) (1982).

Rozin, P. (1990) 'Social and Moral Aspects of Food and Eating', in Rock (ed.) (1990).

Rudat, K. (1992) 'MORI Research – Attitudes to Food, Health and Nutrition Messages among Consumers and Health Professionals', in Buttriss (ed.) (1992).

Russell, G. (1995) 'Anorexia Nervosa Through Time', in Szmukler *et al.* (eds) (1995).

Ryan, D. *et al.* (1982) 'Engel Curves for Meat Consumption in Australia', *Australian Economic Papers*, vol. 21, no. 38, June, pp. 106–22.

Sanderson, M. and J. Winkler (1983) 'Implementing the NACNE Report, Strategies for Implementing NACNE Recommendations', *The Lancet*, 10 Dec., pp. 1353–4.

Sands, R. *et al.* (1997) 'Disordered Eating Patterns, Body Image, Self-Esteem, and Physical Activity in Preadolescent School Children', *International Journal of Eating Disorders*, vol. 21, no. 2, pp. 159–66.

Sanftner, J. *et al.* (1995) 'The Relation of Shame and Guilt to Eating Disorder Symptomatology', *Journal of Social and Clinical Psychology*, vol. 14, no. 4, pp. 315–24.

Sayers, S. (1994) 'Moral Values and Progress', *New Left Review*, no. 204, Mar./Apr., pp. 67–85.

Scarano, G. and C. Kalodner-Martin (1994) 'A Description of the Continuum of Eating Disorders – Implications for Intervention and Research', *Journal of Counseling and Development*, vol. 72, no. 4, pp. 356–61.

Schafer, R. *et al.* (1994) 'The Effects of Marital Interaction, Depression and Self-Esteem on Dietary Self-Efficacy among Married Couples', *Journals of Applied Social Psychology*, vol. 24, no. 24, pp. 2209–22.

Schapira, D. *et al.* (1990) 'The Value of Current Information', *Preventive Medicine*, vol. 19, pp. 45–53.

Schneider, J. *et al.* (1995) 'Gender, Sexual Orientation, and Disordered Eating Behavior', *Psychology and Health*, vol. 10, no. 2, pp. 113–28.

Schucker, R. *et al.* (1992) 'Nutrition Shelf-Labeling and Consumer Purchase Behavior', *Journal of Nutrition Education*, vol. 22, no. 2, pp. 75–81.

Scoppola, M. (1995) 'Multinationals and Agricultural Policy in the EC and USA', *Food Policy*, vol. 20, no. 1, pp. 11–25.

Scott, D. (ed.) (1988) *Anorexia Nervosa and Bulimia Nervosa: Practical Approaches*, London: Croom Helm.

Scott, V. and A. Worsley (1994) 'Ticks, Claims, Tables and Food Groups – A Comparison for Nutrition Labeling', *Health Promotion International*, vol. 9, no. 1, pp. 27–37.

Scottish Office (1993) *The Scottish Diet: Report of a Working Party to the Medical Officer for Scotland*, Edinburgh: The Scottish Office Home and Health Department.

Scourfield, J. (1995) 'Anorexia Nervosa by Proxy: Are the Children of Anorexic Mothers an At-Risk Group?', *International Journal of Eating Disorders*, vol. 18, no. 4, pp. 371–4.

Sen, A. (1981) *Poverty and Famines*, Oxford: Clarendon Press.

Sharma, R. *et al.* (1996) 'An Overview of Assessments of the Impact of the Uruguay Round on Agricultural Prices and Incomes', *Food Policy*, vol. 21, no. 4–5, pp. 351–63.

Sharp, C. (1993) 'Anorexia-Nervosa and Depression in a Woman Blind since the Age of Nine Months', *Canadian Journal of Psychiatry*, vol. 38, no. 7, pp. 469–71.

Sheiham, A. (1991) 'Barriers to Healthy Eating', *The Food Magazine*, April/June, pp. 18–19.

Sheiham, A. *et al.* (1990) 'Recipes for Health', in Jowell *et al.* (eds) (1990).

Shepherd, R. and L. Stockley (1986) 'The Role of Attitudes and Nutritional Knowledge in Fat Consumption', *Proceedings of the Nutrition Society*, vol. 45, no. 1, p. A44.

Silverman, J. (1995) 'History of Anorexia Nervosa', in Brownell and Fairbairn (eds) (1995).

Sjostrom, L. (1993) 'Impacts of Body Weight, Body Composition, and Adipose Tissue Distribution on Morbidity and Mortality', in Stunkard and Wadden (eds) (1993).

Slattery, J. (1986) *Diet Health: Food Industry Initiatives*, University of Bradford: Food Policy Research Unit.

Smith, R. (1993) 'Eating Disorders and the Production–Consumption Dialectic', *New Ideas in Psychology*, vol. 11, no. 1, pp. 95–104.

Smuts, R. (1992) 'Fat, Sex, Class, Adaptive Flexibility, and Cultural Change', *Ethology and Sociobiology*, vol. 13, no. 5–6, pp. 523–42.

Sobal, J. (1995) 'The Medicalization and Demedicalization of Obesity', in Sobal and Maurer (eds) (1995).

REFERENCES

Somogyi, J. and E. Koskinen (eds) (1990) *Nutritional Adaptation to New Life-Styles*, Basel: Karger.

Speed, B. (1995) 'Perspectives on Eating Disorders', *Journal of Family Therapy*, vol. 17, no. 1, pp. 1–11.

Spurr, G. (1990) 'The Impact of Chronic Undernutrition on Physical Work Capacity and Daily Energy Expenditure', in Harrison and Waterlow (eds) (1990).

Spurrell, E. *et al.* (1997) 'Age of Onset for Binge Eating: Are There Different Pathways to Binge Eating?', *International Journal of Eating Disorders*, vol. 21, no. 1, pp. 55–65.

Stare, F. (1976) 'Food Faddisms', in Walcher *et al.* (eds) (1976).

Stein, D. (1991) 'The Prevalence of Bulimia: A Review of the Empirical Literature', *Journal of Nutrition Education*, vol. 23, no. 5, pp. 205–13.

Stein, D. and W. Laakso (1988) 'Bulimia: A Historical Retrospective', *International Journal of Eating Disorders*, vol. 7, no. 2, pp. 201–10.

Stigler, G. and G. Becker (1977) '*De Gustibus Non Est Disputandum*', *American Economic Review*, vol. 67, no. 2, pp. 76–90.

Strak, J. and W. Morgan (eds) (1995) *The UK Food and Drink Industry: A Sector by Sector Economic and Statistical Analysis*, Northborough: Euro PA and Associates.

Striegelmoore, R. *et al.* (1995) 'Drive for Thinness in Black and White Pre-Adolescent Girls', *International Journal of Eating Disorders*, vol. 18, no. 1, pp. 56–69.

Strychar, I. *et al.* (1993) 'Changes in Knowledge and Food Behavior Following a Screening-Program Held in a Supermarket', *Canadian Journal of Public Health*, vol. 84, no. 6, pp. 382–8.

Stunkard, A. and T. Wadden (eds) (1993) *Obesity: Theory and Therapy*, New York: Raven Press, second edition.

Suzuki, K. *et al.* (1995) 'Coprevalence of Bulimia with Alcohol Abuse and Smoking among Japanese Male and Female High School Students', *Addiction*, vol. 90, no. 7, pp. 971–6.

Swann, D. (1995) *The Economics of the Common Market: Integration in the European Union*, London: Penguin, eighth edition.

Swinbank, A. (1993) 'CAP Reform, 1992', *Journal of Common Market Studies*, vol. 31, no. 3, Sept., pp. 359–72.

Swinbank, A. (1994) 'The EC's Policies and Its Food', in Burnett and Oddy (eds) (1994), reproduced from *Food Policy*, vol. 17, no. 1, Feb., pp. 53–64.

Swinbank, A. and C. Tanner (1996) *Farm Policy and Trade Conflict: The Uruguay Round and CAP Reform*, Ann Arbor: University of Michigan Press.

Swinnen, J. and F. van der Zee (1993) 'The Political Economy of Agricultural Policies: A Survey', *European Review of Agricultural Economics*, vol. 20, no. 3, pp. 261–90.

Szmukler, G. and G. Patton (1995) 'Sociocultural Models of Eating Disorders', in Szmukler *et al.* (eds) (1995).

Szmukler, G. *et al.* (eds) (1995) *Handbook of Eating Disorders: Theory, Treatment and Research*, Chichester: John Wiley.

Szymanski, L. and T. Cash (1995) 'Body-Image Disturbances and Self-Discrepancy Theory: Expansion of the Body-Image Ideals Questionnaire', *Journal of Social and Clinical Psychology*, vol. 14, no. 2, pp. 134–46.

Szymanski, L. and R. Seime (1997) Re-Examination of Body Image Distortion: Evidence Against a Sensory Explanation', *International Journal of Eating Disorders*, vol. 21, no. 2, pp. 175–80.

Tansey, G. and T. Worsley (1995) *The Food System: A Guide*, London: Earthscan.

Taras, H. and M. Gage (1995) 'Advertised Foods on Children's Television', *Archives of Pediatrics and Adolescent Medicine*, vol. 149, no. 6, pp. 649–52.

Temple, N. and D. Burkitt (eds) (1994) *Western Diseases: Their Dietary Prevention and Reversibility*, Totawa, NJ: Humania Press.

Thelen, M. *et al.* (1992) 'Eating and Body-Image Concerns among Children', *Journal of Clinical and Child Psychology*, vol. 21, no. 1, pp. 41–6.

Thomas, J. (1979) 'The Relationship between Knowledge about Food and Nutrition and Food Choice', in Turner (ed.) (1979).

Thompson, B. (1992) '"A Way Outa No Way": Eating Problems among African-Americans, Latina, and White Women', *Gender and Society*, vol. 6, no. 4, pp. 546–61.

Thompson, S. (1993) *Eating Disorders: A Guide for Health Professionals*, London: Chapman and Hall.

Thomson, D. (ed.) (1989) *Food Acceptability*, London: Elsevier.

Thompson, S. *et al.* (1997) 'Ideal Body Size Beliefs and Weight Concerns of Fourth-Grade Children', *International Journal of Eating Disorders*, vol. 21, no. 3, pp. 279–84.

Tobin, D. *et al.* (1992) 'Cooperative Relationships between Professional Societies and the Food Industry: Opportunities or Problems?', *Nutrition Reviews*, vol. 50, no. 10, pp. 300–6.

Towler, G. and R. Shepherd (1990) 'Development of a Nutritional Knowledge Questionnaire', *Journal of Human Nutrition and Dietetics*, vol. 3, pp. 255–64.

Turner, B. (1982) 'The Government of the Body: Medical Regimens and the Rationalization of Diet', *British Journal of Sociology*, vol. 33, no. 2, June, pp. 254–69.

Turner, B. (1987) *Medical Power and Social Knowledge*, London: Sage Publications.

Turner, M. (ed.) (1979) *Nutrition and Lifestyles*, London: BNF.

Turner, S. and R. Ingle (eds) (1985) *New Developments in Nutrition Education*, Paris: UNESCO.

Vail, D. *et al.* (1994) *The Greening of Agricultural Policy: Swedish Reforms in Comparative Perspective (Food Systems in Agrarian Change)*, Ithaca, NY: Cornell University Press.

van den Berghe, P. (1984) 'Ethnic Cuisine: Culture in Nature', *Ethnic and Racial Studies*, vol. 7, no. 3, July, pp. 387–97.

van den Broucke, S. *et al.* (1995) 'Marital Intimacy in Patients with an Eating Disorder: A Controlled Self-Report Study', *British Journal of Clinical Psychology*, vol. 34, no. 1, pp. 67–78.

van den Heede, F. and S. Pelican (1995) 'Reflections on Marketing as an Inappropriate Model for Nutrition Education', *Journal of Nutrition Education*, vol. 27, no. 3, pp. 141–5.

van Deth, R. and W. Vandereycken (1995) 'Was Late Nineteenth-Century Nervous Vomiting an Early Variant of Bulimia Nervosa?', *History of Psychiatry*, vol. 6, no. 3(23), pp. 333–48.

Varney, W. (1996) 'The Briar around the Strawberry Patch: Toys, Women, and Food', *Women's Studies International Forum*, vol. 19, no. 3, pp. 267–76.

Viswanath, K. *et al.* (1993) 'Motivation and the Knowledge Gap – Effects of a Campaign to Reduce Diet-Related Cancer Risk', *Communication Research*, vol. 20, no. 4, pp. 546–63.

Walcher, D. *et al.* (eds) (1976) *Food, Man and Society*, New York: Plenum Press.

Walker, C. (1983) Implementing the NACNE Report, The New British Diet', *The Lancet*, 10 Dec., pp. 1354–6.

Walker, C. and G. Cannon (1985) *The Food Scandal: What's Wrong with the British Diet and How to Put It Right*, London: Century.

Walker, L. (1994) 'The Uruguay Round and Agriculture: How Real Are the Gains?', *Review of African Political Economy*, vol. 21, no. 62, Dec., pp. 539–58.

Wallace, B. *et al.* (1993) 'Nutrition Claims in Advertising: A Study of Four Women's Magazines', *Journal of Nutrition Education*, vol. 25, no. 5, pp. 227–35.

Waller, G. and J. Shaw (1994) 'The Media Influences on Eating Problems', in Dolan and Gittinger (eds) (1994).

Warde, A. (1997a) *Consumption, Food and Taste*, London: Sage Publications.

Warde, A. (1997b) 'Review of Fine *et al.* (1996)', *British Journal of Sociology*, vol. 48, no. 2, pp. 328–9.

Waterlow, J. (1990) 'Mechanisms of Adaptation to Low Energy Intakes', in Harrison and Waterlow (eds) (1990).

Weiner, K. and J. Thompson (1997) 'Overt and Covert Sexual Abuse: Relationship to Body Image and Eating Disturbance', *International Journal of Eating Disorders*, vol. 22, no. 3, pp. 273–84.

Wells, M. (1996) *Strawberry Fields: Politics, Class, and Work in Californian Agriculture*, Ithaca, NY: Cornell University Press.

West, R. (1994) *Obesity*, London: Office of Health Economics.

Whichelow, M. (1988) 'Which Foods Contain Dietary Fibre? The Beliefs of a Random Sample of the British Population', *European Journal of Clinical Nutrition*, vol. 42, pp. 945–51.

Whitehead, A. (1994) 'Food Symbolism, Gender Power and the Family', in Harriss-White and Hoffenberg (eds) (1994).

Wilfley, D. and J. Rodin (1995) 'Cultural Influences on Eating Disorders', in Brownell and Fairbairn (eds) (1995).

Wilkins, M. (1994) 'When and Why Brand Names in Food and Drink', in Jones and Morgan (eds) (1994).

Wiseman, M. (1990) 'Government: Where Does Nutrition Policy Come From?', *Proceedings of the Nutrition Society*, vol. 49, pp. 397–401.

REFERENCES

Wolf, N. (1991) *The Beauty Myth: How Images of Beauty Are Used against Women*, London: Chatto and Windus.

Wood, R. (1995) *The Sociology of the Meal*, Edinburgh: Edinburgh University Press.

Wren, B. and B. Lask (1993) 'Aetiology', in Lask and Bryant-Waugh (eds) (1993).

Wright, G. (1990) 'Understanding the UK Food Consumer', *Journal of Marketing Management*, vol. 6, no. 2, pp. 77–86.

Wright, G. and N. Howcroft (1992) *Sources of Information on Diet and Health*, Bradford: Horton Publishing.

Zelizer, V. (1994) *The Social Meaning of Money*, New York: Basic Books.

Ziolko, H. (1996) 'Bulimia Nervosa: A Historical Outline', *International Journal of Eating Disorders*, vol. 20, no. 4, pp. 345–58.

INDEX

Achterberg, C. 89
Adams, L. 89
additives 93, 94
advertising 11, 26, 120; eating
    disorders and 49, 50, 54,
    130n67; and food information
    61, 64, 65, 67, 69, 70, 71, 75,
    76, 78, 79, 80–1, 82, 84, 85,
    86, 87, 93, 135n43; Norway
    115
affluent societies 1–2; *see also*
    diseases of affluence
agricultural policy: and diet
    96–115; Food Standards Agency
    and 12, 116–20; Norway 11,
    96–7, 108–15, 119; *see also*
    Common Agricultural Policy
agriculture 3; productivity 1, 6, 26;
    see also agricultural policy
Alberto-Fidanza, A. 122n5
Andersen, A. 130n67
Anderson, A. 69
Anderson, E. 123n27
Andrews, B. 125n20, 126n30
anorexia nervosa 10, 23, 29–49
    passim, 53, 55
anthropology 90; and anorexia
    130n70; of eating 15
Area Health Authorities *see* Health
    Authorities/Boards
Arnold, E. 40
Arpelagos, G. 15
Ashwell, M. 62, 64, 132n6
Axelson, M. 89

baby feeding information 74
Banks, C. 129n54
Beardsworth, A. 5, 65
Becker, G. 25, 33
Bemporad, J. 44
Biener, L. 30
Biocca, F. 53
Black, A. 133n19
Blaxter, K. 6
Bleau, R. 126n34
BNF *see* British Nutrition
    Foundation
body image 31, 34, 36–8, 39, 40,
    43, 47, 53–6
Bonnano, A. 4
Booth, D. 66
Bordo, S. 43, 90, 124n14, 125n18,
    127n38, 131n72
Bowyer, C. 55, 129n63
Bradby, H. 132n17
Brandtzaeg, B. 113
Bray, A. 45
Brett, April 74
Brinberg, D. 89
British Nutrition Foundation 63,
    64, 67
Brooks, J. 136n7
Brownell, K. 30, 41, 129n62
Brumberg, J. 49, 51, 129n59
Brun, J. 88
Budd, J. 58–9
bulimia 10, 23, 29, 30, 34, 35, 40,
    42, 43, 125n20
Burghardt, R. 20
Burkitt, D. 132n5

Butler, N. 39, 40
Button, E. 41

Calnan, M. 23
Campbell, P. 45
Campbell, T. 75–6
cancer 36, 59, 132n5
Cannon, G. 63
Cantor, J. 54
CAP *see* Common Agricultural Policy
capitalism 6, 37, 47, 51, 56
Caplan, P. 5
Card, M. 127n37
Casson, M. 133n27
Caswell, J. 65, 134n34
Cawley, D. 99, 103–5, 106, 108
Chapman, G. 65
Chernin, K. 24
children: and eating disorders 30, 40, 130n67; and food information 84, 132n13
choice of foods 2–3, 5, 6, 11, 23, 27; determinants 19, 68; food supply and 60; informed, advocated in White Paper on FSA 119–20; relationship of education/information to 10–11, 12, 19, 59, 61, 66, 68, 69, 70
cholesterol 59
Clark, K. 89
coal industry 118
Colditz, G. 124n5
Cole-Hamilton, I. 132n16
Coles, A. 30
COMA *see* Committee on Medical Aspects of Food
comfort eating 39
commercial interests: and food information *see* food information system; and food policy in Norway 109–15; Food Standards Agency and future of food policy 116–20; pressures to eat and to diet 24, 46–57, 85; *see also* advertising
commercialisation of food 21–2, 47
Committee on Medical Aspects of Food Policy report on Diet and

Cardiovascular Disease (COMA) 59, 73
Common Agricultural Policy (CAP) 11, 96, 97–108, 120
compulsion to diet and to eat 10, 42–3, 49, 51, 53; *see also under* commercial interests
consumer: expenditure on food 18, 24–7; and food standards 116–20; ill-health 28–9; responsibility for health *see* individual responsibility; *see also* choice of foods; consumption
consumer demand 2, 72–3, 93–4
consumer groups 92–3; *see also* food activists
Consumers International 134n36
consumption 3, 5, 6, 90, 109; commercial pressures to eat and not eat 24, 46–57, 85; deviancy in *see* eating disorders; economic analysis of 24–7, 32–5; effect of CAP on 96, 97–108; literature 13–18; organically based literature 18–24; systems of provision approach 8
control of body 34, 36, 42, 43, 45, 49, 53
Cooper, C. 125n23
coronary heart disease *see* heart disease
Cosford, P. 40
counter-culture 131n72
counterfactual analysis of CAP 103–8
Crago, M. 40
Crandall, C. 125n23
culture: of food 111; of nutrition 15; *see also* sociocultural factors
current human nutrition thinking (CHNT) 59, 76, 80, 85, 93; and trickle-down model 62–8, 88, 91, 94

dairy products: CAP 98, 106, 107; eating disorders and 55–6; Norway 96–7, 111, 112–14
dairy system 4, 6, 107–8
Davis, C. 40, 127n37

Delahoyde, M. 121n2, 134n36
delocalisation of food provision
    21–2
demand theory 25–6, 32–3, 34
Department of Education and
    Employment 64
Department of Health 63, 116,
    117; Nutrition Unit 60
Department of Health and Social
    Security 63, 67
Despenich, S. 121n2, 134n36
Devine, C. 39, 65
Didomenico, L. 130n67
diet: agricultural policy and
    96–115; economic approach
    24–7; Food Standards Agency
    and 12, 119–20; meanings of
    word 16; nutritional studies
    18–21, 27; paradox of 10, 13–27;
    relationship to information
    see healthy eating information;
    paradox of 10, 13–27;
dieting: compulsion to see
    compulsion to diet and to eat;
    eating disorders and 29–57
    passim; literature review 23–4
dieting industry 30, 31, 49, 51, 52,
    54–6
Dietz, T. 66
diseases of affluence 2, 13, 28, 36,
    57, 59, 63, 109, 110
Domel, S. 132n14
Douglas, M. 15
Driscoll, R. 40
Durkheim, E. 32

eating 7, 90; anthropology of 15; see
    also compulsion to diet and to
    eat
eating diseases see diseases of
    affluence
eating disorders 10, 23–4, 28–57,
    65, 85, 90, 119; applying
    political economy to 31–5, 46;
    incidence 29–30; introducing
    socioeconomic approach 43–57;
    literature about nature of 35–43
economics: of CAP 101, 103–8;
    and eating disorders 31–5; of

food 13, 18, 24–7; see also
    socioeconomic approach
Elias, N. 49
Emmons, L. 127n38
emotions and food 5, 16, 39
Engel's Law 18, 24–7
environment 13
Esler, I. 126n31
ESRC Nation's Diet Programme 2
ethics: of food claims 81; and
    vegetarianism 65
European Union: nutritional policy
    61; see also Common
    Agricultural Policy
expenditure on food 18, 24–7

Falk, P. 130n70
Fallows, S. 73
Farb, P. 15
farming industry see agriculture
fashion industry 51, 52, 56
fat consumption 73, 81, 96, 109
feedback effects 112, 115, 137n22
feminism 43–4, 51, 126n28
fetishism 45
fibre 59, 73, 132n5
Fiddes, N. 22
Fine, B. 2, 6, 8, 9, 17, 32, 46, 49,
    56, 107, 108, 129n58, 136n15
Fischler, C. 16, 21
Fitzgibbon, M. 124n8
food: beliefs about 10, 11, 18, 23,
    132n1; contamination of 28 (see
    also health and safety); costs, and
    choice of diet 67–8; creation of
    meanings and activities around
    3, 5, 39, 50, 55, 65–6;
    distinctive attributes 8–9 (see
    also organic content of food);
    entitlement to 1; political
    economy and eating disorders
    47, 48–53; problematic nature
    of 1–2; quality 13; roles related
    to 39, 65; theoretical approaches
    2–9; variety 2
food activists 92, 93, 94, 117, 120
Food and Drink Federation 93
food and drink industry see food
    industry

food fads 23
food hygiene *see* health and safety of food
food industry: and CAP 107; and eating disorders 48–53; and Food Standards Agency 116; food systems approach 4; healthy eating information 64–8, 71–87, 91, 92–5, 111; *see also* commercial interests
food information system 10–11, 19, 58–95; collaboration between nutritionists and commerce 79–82; critique of literature and proposal of alternative theory 88–91; double duality in 76–9, 84, 92; interaction with food systems 11, 19, 54, 60, 67, 70, 85, 88, 90, 91, 94, 120; literature 60–2; role to be played by nutritional education 68–76; and trickle-down of knowledge 12, 62–8, 88, 91, 94, 120; unfolding theory of healthy eating 61, 76, 77, 82–7
food norms 2–3
food policy 9, 11–12, 28, 116–20; and eating disorders 29, 57; Norwegian attempt to integrate healthy eating with agricultural policy 11, 96–7, 108–15, 119; nutritional studies and 18, 95; *see also* healthy eating policy
Food Policy Research 73
food scares 22, 28, 65, 118–19
Food Standards Agency 12, 116–20
food studies: as a discipline 11, 17, 27; literature review 9–10, 13–27; theoretical approach 2–9
food supply 1–2, 8, 20, 24, 67–8, 106; health and safety 3, 12, 28–9, 109, 118, 120
food system(s): conflicts of interest 118–20; identifying 9; and ill-health 29; interaction with food information system 11, 19, 54, 60, 67, 70, 85, 88, 90, 91, 94, 120; unfolding theory of food information 85
food systems approach 3–9; to CAP 102, 106–8; to eating disorders 10, 57; to nutritional policy 111–12; used to review literature 9–10, 13–27
Foster, G. 23
Foucault, M. 44–5, 90, 122n12
Frederick, C. 126n29
Freeman, C. 127n37
French, J. 89
French, S. 34, 40, 124n8
Freud, S. 42
Friedman, M. 41
Furnham, A. 40

Gage, M. 134n36
Gamman, L. 45
Gardner, B. 98, 103, 135n1, 136n14
Garrett, C. 45
GATT, Uruguay Round 101, 102
Gibney, M. 132n16
Gibson, L. 71
Gillespie, A. 65, 88
Girvin, B. 136n7
Glanz, K. 135n40
Glennie, P. 6
Goldberg, J. 64
Gordon, R. 48
Gormley, T. 92–3
Gosden, H. 73
government policy *see* agricultural policy; food policy; healthy eating policy; regulation of food
grain consumption 1
Gresham's Law 82
Griffiths, R. 136n7
Grivetti, L. 15
Gross, J. 15
Grow, V. 126n29
Guthrie, H. 67, 69, 72

Habermas, J. 44, 45, 78
Hall, P. 40
Harper, A. 75, 76
Harrison, K. 54
Harriss, B. 20

health: beliefs about 18, 65; and
  identity 5; literature about food
  and 13, 23; *see also* ill-health
health and safety of food 3, 12,
  28–9, 90, 109; FSA and 118,
  120
Health Authorities/Boards 64, 71,
  74
health claims, commercial 64, 65,
  71–6, 79, 80–1, 91; unfolding
  theory 82–7
health education 58–9, 89–90; *see
  also* healthy eating information
Health Education Authority 59,
  64, 68, 120
Health Education Council 63, 67,
  72, 73, 135n43
health professionals 63, 75
healthy eating, obstacles to 19
healthy eating campaigns 19, 63,
  64, 66, 96–7, 111, 114–15
healthy eating information 2,
  10–11, 28–9, 59–95;
  commercial and non-commercial
  76–82; critique of literature and
  alternative theory of 88–91; role
  to be played by nutritional
  information 68–76; trickle-
  down model 12, 62–8, 88, 91,
  94, 120; unfolding theory 61,
  76, 77, 82–7
healthy eating policy 18–19, 59,
  60–2, 63, 71, 94–5; FSA and
  12, 119, 120; Norwegian
  attempt to combine with
  agricultural policy 11, 96–7,
  108–15, 119
heart disease 28, 36, 59, 96, 113
Heasman, M. 2, 55
Heaton, A. 30
Henderson, L. 65, 130n68
Hesse-Biber, S. 45, 53
Hetherington, M. 126n35
Hill, A. 37
Hill, B. 100–1
Hill, G. 84
Hill, M. 114
Holm, L. 132n13
Hopwood, C. 45

identity 5, 14–15, 21–2, 45
ill-health, and food 28–9; mental
  29, 35–6; *see also* eating
  disorders; health; psychological
  stress
individual responsibility 58, 60–2,
  70, 78, 110, 120
infant feeding information 74
*International Journal of Eating
  Disorders* 125n15, 128n49
international trade negotiations,
  and CAP 101, 102, 103
Ippolito, P. 79, 82–7, 88

Jackson, L. 25
James, P. 63
James Report (1997) 118–19,
  137n1
Jansen, A. 55
Jansson, S. 66
Japan, agricultural policy 97, 98
Jarman, M. 45
Jeffery, R. 124n8
Jensen, T. 113, 114
Jerome, N. 23
Johnson, D. 103
Johnson, T. 125n23
Joiner, T. 126n26

Kaferstein, F. 23
Kalodner-Martin, C. 124n14
Karagiannis, G. 25
Keane, A. 119, 120, 135n42
Keil, T. 5, 65
Kelder, S. 132n13
Kemm, J. 66
Khandelwal, S. 40
Kirk, T. 79–82
Kirschenbaum, D. 124n8
Kjaernes, U. 109, 113
Kotz, K. 134n36

labelling and packaging 61, 64, 65,
  67, 70, 71, 74, 76, 78, 79,
  80–1, 85, 93, 133n19
Labour Party/Government 116,
  118
Lahiri, S. 25
Lancaster, K. 123n26

Lang, T. 137n4
Lask, B. 41
Leachwood, P. 23
Lee, S. 129n55
Lefebvre, R. 77, 78
Leopold, E. 8
Lester, R. 44
Lobstein, T. 74–5
local food health policies (LFHPs)
    71
local government 117
Lowe, M. 129n55
Lupton, D. 5, 22, 127n43

McCluney, J. 75
McCron, R. 58–9
Macdiarmid, J. 126n35
McKie, L. 65, 133n24
MacLean, H. 65
McManus, K. 69, 70
MacSween, M. 44, 48, 130n71
MAFF see Ministry of Agriculture,
    Fisheries and Food
Makinen, M. 45
malnutrition 2, 20, 95
Malson, H. 45
Malthusianism 1
Martz, D. 128n48
mass communication research 58–9
Mathios, A. 79, 82–7, 88
Mayhew, M. 95
meal, sociology of 6–8
meat: CAP and 106; as symbol 22
meat industry 81, 134n36
meat system 4, 6, 107–8
media: attitude to EU 97, 102;
    and eating behaviour 13, 37,
    53–4, 124n15; and healthy
    eating 64, 73, 84, 86, 92, 93,
    94; see also advertising
media studies 90–1
Mennell, S. 13, 14, 49, 122n12,
    127n45
mental health, and eating disorders
    29, 35–6
Milio, N. 113, 114
Ministry of Agriculture, Fisheries
    and Food (MAFF) 12, 60, 61,
    64, 116–17

Mooney, C. 67–8
Moore, M. 123n21
Morgan, W. 4
Morley, D. 90–1
Murcott, A. 8
Murnen, S. 127n39
Murphy, A. 132n13
Myers, P. 53

Naik, N. 123n21
nation-state 4
National Advisory Committee on
    Nutrition Education (NACNE)
    59, 72–3, 132n16
National Food Survey (NFS) 2
natural attributes of food see organic
    content of food
neoclassical economics see
    economics
Nestle, M. 83, 114
network theory 110
Nichols, S. 70
norms see food norms; nutritional
    norms; social norms
Norway, attempts to coordinate
    agricultural and health
    education policy 11, 96–7,
    108–15, 119
nutrition 13; anorexics and 55;
    culture of 15
nutritional information/education
    see healthy eating information
nutritional norms 19, 21, 22
nutritional policy see healthy eating
    policy
nutritional science/research 63, 64,
    71, 76, 92, 109
nutritional studies of food 18–21,
    27

obesity 10, 29–30, 35, 37–8, 40,
    41, 42, 43, 45, 47, 51, 125n18,
    130n67
O'Connor, T. 75–6
Olson, C. 39, 65
Orbach, S. 34, 48
organic content of food 8–9, 10,
    17, 18–24, 25, 26, 27, 107
overconsumption 47, 48, 109, 111

overeating 31, 35, 38

packaging *see* labelling and packaging
Padberg, D. 65, 134n34
Patel, R. 40
Patton, G. 30, 127n38
Pelican, S. 78
Pelto, G. 21
Pelto, P. 21
Pike, K. 126n31
policy *see* agricultural policy; food policy; healthy eating policy
postmodernism 13
power, food and 4, 45, 78, 90, 122n12
preservation of food 9
pressure groups 92–3; *see also* food activists
Pritchard, W. 4
psychiatry 29, 35
psychological stress, and eating disorders 23–4, 31, 34, 36–43, 46–8
psychology: and eating disorders 29, 35; of food 15, 16
public/private aspects of food information 60

Rayner, M. 133n19
Recommended Daily Allowance 20
regulation of food 28, 29, 70, 71; FSA and 116; health claims 75–6, 85
religious anorexia 44
Rennie, D. 90
Richardson, D. 15
Richardson, N. 65
Riska, E. 137n18
Ritson, C. 106
ritual, eating disorders as 45
Robbins, C. 132n15
Robertson, N. 6
Robinson, T. 130n67
Robison, J. 30, 124n6
Rodin, J. 30, 40
Romeo, F. 48
Rothblum, E. 30, 37, 125n15
Rozin, P. 22, 130n70

Rudat, K. 63
Rudd, J. 135n40
Russell, G. 30, 33
Ryan, D. 25

salt consumption 109
Sanderson, M. 72, 131n2, 132n15, 135n43
Sanftner, J. 125n20
Sayers, S. 28
Scarano, G. 124n14
Schafer, R. 126n36
Schapira, D. 133n20
Schneider, J. 40
Schucker, R. 83
Scoppola, M. 136n10
Scottish Office 111–12
sexual abuse, and eating disorders 38
sexuality, relation to eating disorders 36, 38, 39, 40
Sharp, C. 40
Sheiham, A. 68, 132n11
Shepherd, R. 68, 133n20
shortages of food 1–2, 114
Sjostrom, L. 126n25
Slattery, J. 73, 74
Smith, R. 128n46
smoking, commercial pressures 52
Smolak, L. 127n39
Smuts, R. 128n46
Sobal, J. 45
social marketing 77–8, 79
social norms 22–3, 37
social science literature/research 35, 90, 119
social theory 13, 14, 90; and eating disorders 10, 44–5
Society for Nutrition Education 88
sociocultural factors 18, 20, 21–2; in eating disorders 10, 35–46 *passim*
socioeconomic approach 3; to eating disorders 31–4, 36, 46–57
sociology: of food 14; of the meal 6–8
standardisation of food 9
staple food 2

starvation 1
state 9; theories of 110; *see also*
    nation-state
Stein, D. 124n9
Stigler, G. 25
Stockley, L. 133n20
Story, M. 134n36
Strak, J. 4
strawberry system 4
sugar consumption 108
sugar system 4, 6, 107–8
Suzuki, K. 126n32
Swinbank, A. 100, 103, 106,
    136n14
Szmukler, G. 30, 127n38, 128n48

Tanner, C. 100, 103, 136n14
Tansey, G. 3
Taras, H. 134n36
Thelen, M. 37
thinness 31, 33, 37, 45, 47, 51,
    53–6
Thomas, J. 133n18
Thompson, B. 38
Thompson, J. 126n30
Thompson, S. 125n19
Thrift, N. 6
Tobin, D. 133n29
Towler, G. 68
transnational corporations 4
transport, example of commercial
    pressure 52–3
trauma, and eating disorders 38–9
trickle-down model of food
    knowledge 12, 62–8, 88, 91,
    94, 120
Turner, B. 32, 122n12, 125n18,
    128n46
Turner, S. 30

unfolding theory of food
    information 61, 76, 77, 82–7
United States of America:
    agricultural support policy 97,
    98, 101; food industry and

healthy eating 114; food policy
    85, 134n32; obesity 29–30
Uruguay Round of GATT 101, 102

van den Berghe, P. 22
van den Broucke, S. 126n31
van den Heede, F. 78
Vargas, L. 21
Varney, W. 121n5
vegetarianism 22, 55, 65, 66,
    134n36
Velentzas, K. 25
Vickers, P. 65, 130n68
vitamins 109

Wadden, T. 30, 129n62
Walker, C. 132n15
Wallace, B. 86
Warde, A. 5, 6
Weiner, K. 126n30
welfarism, and nutritional policy
    110
Wells, M. 40
West, R. 30
Whichelow, M. 133n21
White Paper on Food Standards
    Agency 116–20, 137n1
Whitehead, A. 126n36
Wilfley, D. 40
Wilkins, M. 133n27
Williams, S. 23
Wilson, M. 125n23
Winkler, J. 72, 131n2, 132n15,
    135n43
Wiseman, M. 60–2, 93
Wolf, N. 126n27
women, and eating disorders 10,
    24, 31–40 *passim,* 46–7, 65
Wood, R. 7, 133n24
Worsley, T. 3
Wren, B. 41
Wright, G. 93–4
Wright, J. 2

Yager, J. 40, 127n37